WILLIAM SHAKESPEARE'S "NAKED"

HAMLET

WILLIAM SHAKESPEARE'S
"NAKED"
HAMLET

A Production Handbook

BY

Joseph Papp

Assisted by TED CORNELL

THE MACMILLAN COMPANY
COLLIER-MACMILLAN LTD., LONDON

CONTENTS

Illustrations
of representative scenes
from the 1968 productions of *Hamlet* by the
New York Shakespeare Festival Public Theater
FOLLOWING PAGE 96

All photographs by George Joseph

"You shall know I am set naked on your kingdom."
—HAMLET'S LETTER TO CLAUDIUS (IV, VII, 43)

Why does Shakespeare send his leading character on a bizarre ocean voyage for almost five hundred lines at the most crucial point of the play and then have him announce his return by a strange letter and tell a most fantastical story of pirates, waxen seals, royal imprimaturs, and death warrants?

These off-stage happenings suggest an expressionistic trip of the mind, a film in super-fast motion going through Hamlet's head, and leads me to believe that Hamlet never leaves Denmark at all but undergoes a transformation allowing him to do what he has to do in the swift and final scenes of the play.

PREFACE

WHAT FOLLOWS IS the text that was used for the 1968 production of *Hamlet* at the New York Shakespeare Festival Public Theater, as rearranged and directed by Joseph Papp. In addition to an essay by the director regarding his approach to the play, there are complete stage directions, diagrams, photographs, and wayside comments to engage the reader and provide him with a sense of the flow of the play on the stage.

Since the true spirit of the theater must be constantly revived by the fresh knownothingness of the amateur, we invite the adventurous reader to "stage" his own production of *Hamlet*, not on the boards, but in his mind's eye. It is particularly useful, therefore, to turn these pages without any preconceived notions of the play. But if you have them, we suggest they be laid to rest for the duration of this reading experience. Afterward you may revise your thinking about this great classic, or be outraged as the gray-haired lady in our audience who said she was "defiled."

Though the *New York Times* critic denigrated the effort and labeled it "a *Hamlet* for the Philistines," the Public Theater was jammed every night for the run of the play, attracting audiences predominantly in their teens and early twenties.

There were some who did not share the enthusiasm of the

youth and regarded the presentation as the beginning of the end of Western civilization. While these were minority expressions, they were extremely vocal.

One furious lady in her seventies accused the production of contributing to the "defiance of teenagers who are already blatantly defiant." She called it "wildly languaged buffoonery for kids who already clown and scoff at any semblance of authority and order." Not to be left out, the superintendent of education called it "a gross distortion of Shakespeare unsuited to the maturity of high school students." Someone else said that "it caused the utter disintegration of regard for constituted authority into which youth eternally erupts." Another lady called it "a complete disaster which left me bored, deaf, blind and definitely uncommitted to a vulgar, noisy and pretentious intellectual production." A Mr. F. exploded with, "This guttersnipe *Hamlet* is worthy of the barracks or a school for delinquents." A well-intentioned Dr. S. wrote: "Is there not some danger in this, the time of the Vietnam War . . . when shooting and killing are made light of in your play? I hope you are not preparing our youth for war in Vietnam." A Mrs. B. called it "a travesty, tasteless and degenerate." And then a Mr. M. remarked: "The *Hamlet* you have done is a perfect example of McLuhanism in action; denigration of the world and sensation for immediacy's sake. Rock and Roll is the only message here." And then finally a Mrs. B., in a flush of Shakespearean erudition, said: "You have one admirer much offended, Mr. Papp, by the present performance which you entitle *Hamlet*. 'O judgment that art fled to brutish beasts and Papp has lost his reason!' 'Yours with rivers in the eyes . . .' " One angry Ukrainian called the production an offense to our fighting men in Vietnam.

On the other side of the ledger, the following comments were made:

Letter to the Editor, *The New York Times*: "What can be more pertinent today than to have a man from a minority group

—Papp chose Puerto Rican—do the 'To be or not to be' soliloquy . . . ? I found myself listening hard to all the words, for they came alive because of the action accompanying them."

Mr. T.: "I think the Puerto Rican soliloquy and the little dialogue that precedes it is one of the most inspired scenes in your marvellously imaginative production."

Miss G.: "I felt you were faithful to Shakespeare's *Hamlet*. The beauty and dynamism, too often lost or overshadowed in the traditional productions . . . was retained and made more understandable because it became so relevant."

Mrs. S.: "I felt that your production . . . did something very personal for me, in the sense that I feel much closer to the young people who are reacting against the institutionalized brutality and hypocrisy of our time—and consequently much closer to my own son."

Mr. R.: "The pure hilarity helps us all as did 'Hells a Poppin' forty years ago—it all does honor to Shakespeare."

Mr. P.: "Though the critics were not very receptive, I am sure that audiences will respond positively, as they did the two times that I saw the show. Please don't 'give up the ship'—we who are sick of dusty, traditional theater uptown relish your enthusiasm, your experiments."

Miss E.: "I saw your *Hamlet* and loved it. I laughed my head off at all those wonderful gags—and what pace and energy it had."

Mr. McD.: "Joseph Papp's work betrayed an important idea; namely, that to produce a great play is to confront not only a great text but also a great tradition. . . . The production as a whole worked *against* recent tradition but *with* the text and subtext. . . . In working against the well-done tragedy, the production made material from which uniquely tragic moments could be carved: firsthand, contemporary, pure, and, as we often say of life, 'unreal.' "

Mr. T.: "Enjoyed your *Hamlet* because of the experimental nature and attempt at freeing the actors. . . . Satire, farce, melodrama, comedy and tragedy were all evident and because the fabric of the play is so rich your attempts at vitalizing it were meaningful."

Mrs. L.: "The modernization of classical plays usually results in inconsistency and absurdity, but your *Hamlet* never came close to tumbling in those two pitfalls."

The *New York Times* drama critic found himself with strange bedfellows: his Sunday colleague, Walter Kerr (who thought the vaudeville was not up to snuff), and the aisle-sitter from the New York *Daily News*—an authentic non-Philistine.

Serious theater critics—Robert Brustein of *The New Republic*, Alan Rich of *Time* Magazine, Emily Genauer, formerly of the New York *Herald-Tribune* and now with *Newsday*, TV critics Len Harris (CBS) and Allen Jefferys (ABC), Michael Smith of the *Village Voice*—had this to say about the production:

> Robert Brustein, the *New Republic*: "I found the whole under-taking to be pretty courageous, and while it has drawn a pre-dictable response from those who prefer their Kulchur pre-packaged, standardized, and wholly digestible like a TV dinner, I think it is bound to have an effect on the theatrical conscious-ness for some time to come. . . . Mr. Papp's group remains, to my mind, the only one in town dedicated not simply to remounting familiar masterpieces but to trying to discover what theater can mean to America in the sixties."
>
> Alan Rich, *Time* Magazine: "A serious attempt to demonstrate the viability of Shakespeare's insights into men's weaknesses in terms of modern theater. This *Hamlet* is a gathering of fantasies envisaged by the leading players . . . emotions are inner, private and unshared, until they clash in a series of brutal, shattering collisions. Shakespeare's language remains undisturbed but Papp's imaginative scissoring and repasting has sculptured a *Hamlet* of crystalline tensity."
>
> Emily Genauer, *Newsday*: "Joseph Papp's new *Hamlet* is a brilliant example of a play not added to but turned inside out. . . . His technical devices have to do with pop art, with bringing on images bigger and more absurd than they are in life itself. They also have to do with cubism, in that he boldly breaks apart characters, speeches, sequences, familiar conceptions, to put them together again in a new and freshly revealing light—or even to leave them fragmented, which can be most revealing of all. . . . It sends shafts of intense light on over-familiar passages."
>
> Leonard Harris, CBS-TV: ". . . raucous, annoying, explosive and exciting. . . . It is both Cubist and Pop. Cubist in that it tries to break the characters down into planes and angles we have never seen before. . . . Pop because it tries to force the art of

Shakespeare to co-exist with modern trappings—and thereby to shake Shakespeare up and to jangle the audience a bit too."

Allen Jefferys, ABC-TV: "This *Hamlet* is one of the most fascinating departures from the traditional I have seen. Once you get used to the strange costumes, this *Hamlet* not only ceases to annoy, it begins to intrigue."

Michael Smith, *Village Voice*: "Joseph Papp has shaken the daylights out of Shakespeare and turned *Hamlet* upside down, cut, scrambled, pared it down, and pasted it back together all out of kilter. . . . It's a hallucinatory *Hamlet*, with the clashing styles, jagged emotional tone, and image overload of specifically the 1960's."

Letter to the Editor, *The New York Times*, from Richard Schechner, Editor of the *Drama Review*: "Like Peter Brook's *Marat/Sade* or the work of Jerzy Grotowski, Mr. Papp's *Hamlet* points toward emerging and liberating forces within the theater. . . . I, for one, welcome the farce, the terror, the lust, the confusion, and the contradictions of this production. How satisfying they are after all the oatmeal the theater usually serves."

Why this wide divergence of opinion? With few exceptions the dissenters were intelligent people; many had supported Free Shakespeare in the Park since its beginnings. Clive Barnes is an erudite gentleman and his reign as drama critic for the *Times* is marked by thoughtful and perceptive comments about the theater. Fortunately, those who disagreed were in the minority, but in numbers not in age. Age seemed to play the decisive role in shaping audience response, though, like Mr. M., there were some older and elderly folk who, with some trepidation, gave themselves to the *Hamlet* experience. Mr. M., who listed his profession as public relations, admitted: "Fascinating conception —prophetic—frightens us (age 45) but not kids."

A student, aged seventeen, demonstrated the aptness of Mr. M.'s remark. He said: "I was amazed at my own capacity to receive such entertainment, instruction, elation. I hate to leave my final comment at something like fantastic, but I'm afraid it'll have to do." Other students, mainly at the college level, had this to say:

"*Hamlet* was an enjoyable evening. I was stunned, shocked, amused, annoyed, and satisfied. Having just studied 'H' in school I was familiar with the deviations. I can't think of an apt Shakespearean quote so I'll just say 'Bravo!' "

"This is really a groovy idea."

"I enjoyed *Hamlet* very much, with a few reservations. It's too bad most of the critics either missed the point or did not appreciate it."

"Good thing Will's dead!"

"It's a wonderful experience to see a play I've studied and read done so well—as if I was a part of it."

"*Hamlet* was superb! I never thought I could enjoy Shakespeare so much. A brilliant production."

"Fantastic. Don't be discouraged by unimaginative critics."

"Who's Clive Barnes?"

"I greatly enjoyed your take-off production. Physically involving the audience so much in the play was something new to me, and, along with the acting, made the characters seem more believable and realistic, rather than just players on a stage. . . . If one of your goals was to make one pause and think about, not take for granted, what is happening on stage—then you have, in my opinion, succeeded."

"Although I have never seen any other productions of *Hamlet*, I found your play very interesting. The changes that were used to bring it up to date made it very timely."

"*Hamlet* was incredible—exciting, shocking, enthralling, demanding, at times disappointing, but fabulous vaudeville."

Aside from one or two professors of English, the great majority of educators at all grade levels and university status made comments of this kind:

"We're always interested in good experimental and repertory theater. We appreciate your desire to try new things—and old plays—in a new way."

"This was not Shakespeare but *some* of Shakespeare's ideas. It was not *Hamlet* but (whatever it could be called) was worth seeing not purely as comedy or tragedy but comment on life."

"Hurrah for this one."

"Keep it up. Thoroughly fun."

"Marvelous, human production."

"My first introduction to your new theater was the production of Hamlet As A Happening. I was very impressed with . . . your attempt with the play. I'm not sure how well you succeeded, but I found the attempt refreshing enough to recommend it to my classes."

"Terrific—More meaningful—Most contemporary."

"I thought this the liveliest *Hamlet* I've seen in years. The contemporary setting and mock-serious attitude gave fresh meaning to those tired old lines. It would be easy to carp over some aspects of the production, but at least you took some risks and created an entertainment, thereby giving me more than my money's worth."

Chairman, high school English department: "I do not recall ever having been so moved and stirred by a dramatic presentation. Your rather daring step in 'tampering' with such a classic as this is more than justified by these results—Shakespeare is proved once again to be our contemporary; this is just the sort of attitude and presentation which is necessary to convince modern theatergoers—particularly the younger ones—that a work of established repute and 'classic' status does not need to be dead or 'textbooky.' To have managed . . . to retain the taste and quality of Shakespeare and still to inject something of the paces and tensions of New York 1967 is an accomplishment of great proportion."

Then there was a broad variety of professionals from all walks of life who responded this way:

Civil engineer: "This is the most creative, imaginative thing I've seen in years—fantastic!"

Editor: "Hamlet has been in my heart of hearts for 8 years. . . . I've seen him dozens of times and nearly memorized him. Tonight I laughed in 50 new places and none of the old ones. Beautiful."

Stock broker: "A precious contribution to New York culture and entertainment. I give you only the highest praise—and *thanks*."

Executive: "*Hamlet* was a 'Gas'!"

Manufacturer's representative: "Best Shakespeare yet!"

New York City Commissioner of Parks: "Your *Hamlet* is *fascinating*—an unforgettable evening of theater."

Nuclear scientist: "Your *Hamlet* is astonishingly good. It is not only good but makes perfect sense also. . . . The whole play was so full of unusual insights that it makes one wish to talk to you and your people."

Artist-painter: "I've found the sense of the production brilliant and the acting too. Ditto for adaptation."

Magazine editor: "Your *Hamlet* is both absorbing and entertaining. I won't say it supplants the Dane with a skull in his hand, but it surely deepens and enriches one's understanding of that figure."

Camp Fire Girls executive: "I am certain if Shakespeare were alive today he would applaud your direction of his *Hamlet* that is so vibrant and timely for our generation."

Administrative assistant: "Enjoy seeing a fresh approach to *Hamlet*. The seriousness usually associated with the play was lacking, but this added to the audience's enjoyment. A nontraditional approach made the audience feel free to have a spontaneous reaction to it."

These impassioned responses to *Hamlet*, both negative and positive, are revealing in many aspects. Understanding them is important to those of us who have created this provoking production, as well as for those who believe in the theater as a unique platform for ideas and human experiences. The search may cast some light on the question of the theater's role in a cinematic and television era.

To end: Jump in—the water's fine!

WILLIAM SHAKESPEARE'S "NAKED"
HAMLET

THE NAKED HAMLET

Hamlet, THE PLAY, is uncomplicated and may be understood without analysis. The story, in fact, is rather corny and melo-dramatic and worthy of a place in Lamb's *Tales.* But one can easily say that there is no story without Hamlet the *character* and that Hamlet *is* the story. If so, then there is no way to direct the play without looking at it through the eyes and the feelings of Hamlet. What does he see? He looks at Elsinore and its in-habitants in the same way Picasso might look at a face or conventional landscape. The characters that people his brain are remolded, recolored, reshaped so that they bear slight resemblance to what they really are. And what are they, really? Nothing but what Hamlet's thinking makes them.

The one sure way of creating a dead fish Hamlet is to impose upon him a consistent line of behavior. There is no bloodier bore of a Hamlet than a melancholy one. Well then, if Hamlet is not melancholy, what is he? The one characteristic most discernible throughout the play can be described in the vernacular of the hippie: he is a "put-onner" and a "put-downer," a master of disguises who has learned the survival method of the death camp. He not only speaks daggers—but uses them. Within the Renaissance perfection of this noble mind rankles that "vicious mole of nature," that one defect, that one particular fault, which corrupts him and causes the deaths of Polonius, Ophelia, Laertes (an entire family), Rosencrantz and Guildenstern, Gertrude and Claudius, and, in the end, Hamlet himself.

In this production Hamlet is the Phantom of the Opera of the silent film—darting along the precarious heights of the theater gridiron, curling up in a nutshell (and accounting himself a king of infinite space). He looms large over all proceedings below him, observing his handiwork—and the forces he has set in motion—with grim delight.

Yet this seeming oddball has one precious possession which he holds to himself—his feelings. While he may show them in various guises, he never reveals the original. While he mocks, he is being mocked. He is both victimizer and victim. He never dreams, because his reality is fantastical and nightmarish. "Perchance to dream?" How may one dream of a dream of a dream and keep his sanity? Hamlet is what he does. Thought and action are one—there is no split. An impulse is an invitation to motion wrapped in words.

In this version Hamlet is unleashed—catapulted and flung into the midst of the court (and the audience), leaving havoc and wreckage in his wake. This is the dynamic that underlies the production. The hoary question, "Is Hamlet a man of action or of words?" has no relevance here. Certainly no one would dare to bring it up in Hamlet's presence. However, with Hamlet out of earshot, this question might be broached: What is the cause of the defect? The answer could be contained in yet another question: Is the death of a father one of the most shattering experiences a son could have? Is the loss of the key male link with the past an irreparable one? Is there fear in the hidden realization that the boy has become the father? Hamlet is "too much i' the sun" and the son is too much in him. So much so that he wants to remain the son in defiance of the reality that, at the death of his father, the boy becomes the man—and has the man's responsibility to fulfill his purpose in nature: to father his own offspring. But Hamlet chooses to remain the eternal son, to hold back the process of nature and live outside the pale of human-kind. He will not be reconciled, and chooses his own death rather than fall in line with the common theme—the death of fathers. He dies a son.

Note how he refuses to be comforted when confronted with the irrefutable logic to cease mourning over the loss of his father:

GERTRUDE: Thou know'st 'tis common, all that lives must die,
  Passing through nature to eternity.
HAMLET: Ay, madam, it is common.
CLAUDIUS: . . . But you must know, your father lost a father;
  That father lost, lost his, and the survivor bound
  In filial obligation for some term
  To do obsequious sorrow. But to persever
  In obstinate condolement is . . .
  A fault against the dead, a fault to nature,
  . . . whose common theme
  Is death of fathers, and who still hath cried,
  From the first corse till he that died today,
  "This must be so."

But it must not be so with Hamlet. He will not be comforted. He will violate the law of nature. He will not accept his loss and go on as though nothing has changed. His intransigence must also deny woman—the other half that might have given him a son. He refuses to alter his role and insists on remaining the son of a father and not the father of a son.

This challengeable psychological premise is the rationale upon which we base Hamlet's erratic mode of existence. We have no need to prove its inviolability. Even if we could, it would have no particular bearing on the performance which is presentational and has no use for psychology. Perhaps it is occasionally and unconsciously reflected in the ache around the audience's heart, or Hamlet's, for that matter:

HAMLET: But thou would'st not think how ill all's here about my
  heart. But it is no matter.

Hamlet is right. It is no matter. Why take cognizance of those black and gnarled primitive roots which reach deeply into the mystical death of fathers? There would be no play. The first scene would be the last, and the audience would demand its money back.

SEARCHING THE TEXT

POLONIUS: If circumstances lead me, I will find
   Where truth is hid, though it were hid indeed
   Within the centre.

LEAR: That way madness lies.

HAMLET: Let us go in together.

One must not approach this play timidly. It is as tough as a coconut, and to crack the crust you must be prepared to bite hard and run the risk of cracking your teeth. But bite you must. The hard shell of the play's inner logic will not yield to scholarship or opportunistic manhandling. The gnashing of teeth, however, must be accompanied by a gently beating heart and a free-floating imagination. The combination of these may permit you to enter the "center" where the mystery lies curled up and waiting to be conjured. You must come as a lover, not mindlessly romantic, but with your blood and judgment well co-mingled so that you meet Hamlet as a living organism, not as a literary abstraction.

Clues to the enigma of Hamlet have been mistakenly sought in the great and familiar soliloquies, based on the notion that Hamlet in his soul-searching reveals the truth of himself. But, as in life, a man does not show himself, or know himself, in beautifully organized eloquence. Since one can die of a scratch as well as of an atom bomb, our search focused on the seemingly insignificant incidents of the play—when there is not great expectation and the audience's guard is down, when the subject on stage is under no pressure to say precisely what he feels.

One such incident occurs at the most crucial point of the play's development, shattering Hamlet's explosive being into thousands of fragments—which throughout the action of the play he unsuccessfully attempts to reunite. I refer to the reappearance of his father, recently murdered by his father's brother. The effect created by this strange meeting of dead father and living son sends the play on its wild and erratic course. All that precedes this meeting—Hamlet's mourning, thoughts of suicide, his profound despair, contempt for womankind, his sardonic interplay with Horatio, his belief that the "vicious mole of nature," the "stamp of one defect," is all his own particular fault—all of this is priming his body for that fantastic jolt which takes him out of this world onto a new plane of reality experienced only by those ready for death—freed of any responsibility. Lucid, clairvoyant, he ignites the air around him, driving him and all of those who come within his electric circle to suicide, madness, or murder.

HORATIO: . . . the dreadful summit of the cliff.

A line, generally passed over, is a key to the planes of reality referred to above:

HAMLET: Remember thee? Ay, thou poor ghost, *while memory holds a seat in this distracted globe.*

This is an antic line, a joke which must have set the Globe Theater audience on a roar. "A seat in this distracted globe"— a laugh line given to the great tragic figure of Hamlet? The separation of tragic and comic actor must have been slight indeed in Shakespeare's company. Was it this same Richard Burbage, now playing the melancholy Dane, who had torn the house down with his Falstaff? By our standards today (and those of the nineteenth century) we are confused when Shakespeare labels *The Merchant of Venice* a comedy. We offer a rather weak explanation—the dividing line is death. But cannot death be an antic? Are *Measure for Measure, The Tempest, All's Well That Ends Well* comedies?

Perhaps we must take a new look at these old sturdy classifications, categorized for literary reference and removed from life. If we dare to do that, we may discover that the style of performing *Hamlet* is far removed from the melancholic and brow-furrowed "classical" standard passed down for generations, making the study of this great work a chore for millions of school children.

What is this distracted globe in which memory holds a seat? The immediate and standard interpretation is—Hamlet's head. Hamlet's globe. But we must not stop here, or we lose the triple play that Shakespeare gives us. The distracted globe is also the world—the globe of the distracted world. And finally it is the Globe Theater and its distracted audience. This richly endowed, three-layered image reveals to us the interaction among Hamlet, his audience (the theater), and the world—all equally distracted. "Taint not thy mind," admonishes the father—but alas, it is a multi-colored mind he is addressing, a mind that he can by no means grasp—which he has never grasped—any more than his wife Gertrude can. This boy's brain is out of their reach.

After the Ghost's disappearance, Hamlet can barely stand up. "Hold, hold my heart," he cries. He vows, he pledges an unswerving commitment to his father's memory—to his commandment. He will be pure in the pursuit: He attacks his mother as pernicious, his uncle as a smiling damned villain—and then suddenly he takes ever so slight a turn: "My tables, my tables! Meet it is I set it down/That one may smile, and smile, and be a villain." He writes it in a book and his pledge for all purposes is now fulfilled. He is high and flying and ecstatically engages Horatio in elusive byplay:

HORATIO: What news, my lord?
HAMLET: O, wonderful!

HORATIO: Good my lord, tell it.

HAMLET: No, you'll reveal it.

HORATIO: Not I, my lord, by heaven!

HAMLET: How say you, then? would heart of man once think it? But you'll be secret?

HORATIO: By heaven, my lord.

HAMLET: An apparition appeared before me with this message—

HORATIO: What message, my lord?

HAMLET: There's ne'er a villain dwelling in all Denmark but he's an arrant knave.

HORATIO: There needs no ghost to tell us this.

HAMLET: Why right; you are in the right; and so, without more circumstances at all, I hold it fit that we shake hands and part; you, as your business and desire shall point you—for every man hath business and desire, such as it is—and, for my own poor part, I will go pray.

HORATIO: These are but wild and whirling words, my lord.

Throughout this scene Hamlet is the antic, perplexing his friend Horatio (and Marcellus and Bernardo) who are caught up in his frenzy. He makes them swear to keep his secret and they do under the combined pressure of the wild prince and his old mole father. From now on, Hamlet is up and away.

Once the decision is made that distraction is the norm, then all the psychological questionings—the why's—become totally irrelevant. This conclusion begins to serve as a liberating force which cuts the play from its nineteenth-century moorings and sends it aloft, free-floating in twentieth-century outer space.

The monumental question of the play, "To be or not to be," needs no investigation in our chosen circumstances. Questions of action or thought are meaningless. The end is always in sight— a poisoned sword, a poisoned cup, and in our text a roulette bullet. All that was required of the director and the company was to invent engaging and interesting devices to sugarcoat the agony of a man living out his short span of life. Why the sugar-coating? Because the truth is unbearable—for the audience as well as for the character and the players. And so we devised burlesque skits, song and dance routines, familiar vaudeville tricks guaranteed to hold the attention of any red-blooded man, woman, or child. Tricks to reveal the truth and to keep the spectator from dozing off, escaping into the syrup of familiar recitations. We found tricks and sketches to reveal the truth in easy doses. With the eradication of the "why," the work process was dictated by "what" and "how." If inadvertently an actor would raise the "why," it was easy enough to strike the questioner dumb with "why not" or "because."

> POLONIUS: What do you read, my lord?
> HAMLET: Words, words, words.

Great works of art are implicitly contradictory because they are the closest representation of life. Life being ambiguous, a work of art reflecting this ambiguity can be approached in a variety of ways, and I'm talking about a play which had a particular life at a particular time. I might go so far as to say that one could, in a particular age, change the viewpoint of the playwright himself, because if the playwright is a great playwright, as Shakespeare was, he makes this possible. *Hamlet* was approached this way. It is a play of contradiction—the breaking down of the "forts and pales of reason." Things are topsy-turvy. Things are turned on their heads.

We can take Hamlet's rational advice to the players, a highly civilized statement, and in light of what has happened since Shakespeare's time and is happening today, we can turn it upside down: "Speak the speech, I pray you, as I pronounced it to you, trippingly on the tongue." Why? Too many speeches have been, and are being, made trippingly on the tongue and they are not to be trusted. "I had as lief the town-crier spoke my lines."

Yes, I had as lief the town crier spoke those lines, for they should be shouted from the rooftops. The air must be sawed with hands—hands have been sawed. Split the ears of the groundlings —ears have been split. In the torrent, tempest, and whirlwind of passion in the world, man seems to be unable to acquire and beget a temperance to give it smoothness. We are tearing ourselves to tatters, to very rags, and we are capable of nothing but inexplicable dumbshows and noise. Discretion is no tutor, and the modesty of nature is stepped over. If we hold, as 'twere, the mirror up to nature, it would be a distorted mirror and a spookhouse of a carnival. Nature's journeymen have made men but not made them well, they imitate humanity so abominably. A thing of beauty is a joy forever. Its loveliness increases. It will never pass into nothingness, but still will keep a bower quiet for us and a sleep full of sweet dreams and health and quiet breathing.

Hamlet—what a wounded name—survivor of wars, cataclysms, and catastrophes. What a piece of work is a man—sprawled in the dirt of Vietnam—on the beaches of Iwo Jima—in the trenches of Verdun—on 125th Street in Harlem—on the streets of Detroit, Newark, Cleveland—in a grave in Alabama that held the remains of Andrew Goodman, civil rights worker—the death of Roosevelt, of Einstein, Marilyn Monroe, and a fourteen-year-old boy in the Bedford-Stuyvesant section of Brooklyn. How noble in reason, infinite in faculty. What is this quintessence of dust? A curiosity of nature, walking upright on two legs while all other creatures crawl or walk on four or six or a hundred. Hamlet, a miracle of nature. A testimony to the stubborn, relentless will to face life and create wonders in the shadow of annihilation. It must be stupidity, for intelligence would have thrown in the sponge a long time ago. The end is finite and yet there is that peculiar instinct for remaining on earth propagating the species, holding on to the hair of hope. This form of mammal incredibly develops the means of its own systematic demise here in a world of chaos that yet can produce poets with flowing mouths, singing great songs of man, hymns to man. It is astounding.

Mountains and trees have a nobility, for they are silent. The dumb beast, wordless, protects its young, prowls the jungles and the plains, eying the muzzle of a gun with yellow looks, suspicious, fearful, and wild. Nature has winds and thunder at its command and deep, turbulent seas swelling and powerful— alive with golden, black, psychedelic, swimming, darting things of fins and gills. It has brilliant flowers and shells and red earth and giant trees and clouds of pink-white, gray-black, and skies and water of the same incredible blue. But this God-Nature, a silent animal, brilliant, beautiful, unpredictable, all-powerful, lacks the one extraordinary human talent—words, words, words.

There is nothing more deceptive than language. It literally undergoes change. Words grow old and are dropped from the vocabulary. Words take on new meanings. Words change as ideas change. What is unchangeable are the symbols underlying the consciousness of words. Human experience remains constant. Love in all its forms reappears in every generation with varied but basically unchanged significance. Words have power. Words must be spoken. Words left unsaid are a form of destruction, of death, of nihilism, of the eradication of the living impulse. Words are treacherous, unpredictable, and have been responsible for mass killings. The world has changed through words. The world will change again through words.

Hamlet is a work of art in which words are formidable and determine the outcome of lives. Words are lancers, bullets, bombs. They are pain and they are pleasure. They are soft. They are hard. They are cruel. They are kind. They are truthful, they are false. *Hamlet* is a play on words. It is word play which leads to sword play. It is so richly endowed with strata and multi-levels of words spoken outright, words thought and words vaguely remembered, that it is possible in this time to rearrange the words, to shatter them, to blow them at the moon and watch them float down into the lives of the characters like so many fragments of living matter and begin to form into new shapes, but within this process not lose the deep continuous symbols underlying them. A masterpiece is powerful and can withstand these shocks to which it is submitted.

It is utterly fantastic to find people reacting to this production of *Hamlet* in almost opposite ways—in totally opposite ways, both pro and con—and yet if these people were to be placed in the same room and asked their opinions and feelings about the war in Vietnam or the question of the survival of the human race, they would, I venture to say, find themselves in total agreement. This is a strange but superb revelation of the nuances of human appreciation or acceptance. What is good for the goose is not necessarily good for the gander. Because of the comfort people have found in a thing of beauty, in what they consider to be a constant in civilization, *Hamlet*, which has withstood great wars and devastation, to view this precious and, what they consider, unchangeable piece of work—to view it from underneath, through the side, through cracks in the sentences, through great chinks in the wall of tradition—creates uncertainty, fear, and doubt and must be denied, as it has been by some.

The play, unloosed from its moorings, requires the viewer to be free-floating, to give himself to space, to go with it, to dig it, to fly fearlessly through the air and turn and twist and stand on his head and his arms and let his hair blow in the wind. This is difficult for those who have committed themselves to the past and hold on to it for dear life. On the other hand there are those—and they are in the great majority of our audience, principally the youth who have not yet been instilled with the knowledge of their ultimate disappearance from this earth—who have the courage and the daring to be free. They have expressed their exhilaration in the experience and have made such extraordinary comments as groovy, wild, sends me—the vernacular of our time; they have, I was going to say, enjoyed it, but they have experienced the insides of a work of art that has grown stale, respectable, and therefore coated with the varnish that prevents the viewer from coming to grips with the real life force within the play.

The process of work this entailed was an unusual experience for both the director and the acting company. Each had to remove his own varnish and make his mind and body free and vulnerable to the wild and darting ideas which prevail in the play, *Hamlet*. Stars were bursting in the sky, the moon was turned upside down, and the walls of the rehearsal hall faded away. There was only the human heart exposed, beating and hungry. *Hamlet* is a crisis-ridden play, and if ever humanity was in a crisis, it is now. But it is not enough to talk in terms of humanity. In order to penetrate the deep, deep, dark recesses of this work, one must find that crisis in himself. All the odds that one feels himself at are brought into play, and it is the relationship of one's own being to that piece of work which makes the search glorious—painful, yet glorious.

A NOTE ON THE TEXT

How DID THE peculiar set of lines and business which you will find in the following pages evolve? The text that was presented to the company at the first rehearsal was already considerably abridged, and the action was set in Fortress Denmark with Claudius, the usurping King, assuming the role of a military dictator. There were as yet no colloquial interpolations, and although there were already some rearrangement of scenes and inter-cutting of speeches, the text retained a strict plot form. The logic of assembling this rehearsal text was not, as is most common, to eliminate certain plot lines, but rather to distill and, if necessary, reassemble the complexities of the text. Often the text focused on apparently less significant sections of dialogue, and as rehearsals progressed, major scenes which were carried intact into the working text were revised or restated so that eventually no scene was allowed to carry the same significance it bears in the classical arrangement.

Rehearsals were a process of unraveling and reweaving the text and the business of the play until the form which you see here was reached. This process continued when the second and then a third production were mounted as new actors and new ideas reshaped the play. The text you see here represents an arbitrary interruption of the continuing process which should be renewed in your production.

We can illustrate the weaving process by picking an arbitrary point in the play and tracing the threads which create it. How, for example, did Ophelia come to make her exit from the vaudeville scene (Scene xxx) in a litter basket?

In the classical text Ophelia sings her mad songs to Gertrude and Claudius and at one point to Laertes. In our first text, these scenes were abridged and condensed into one scene which Hamlet played with Ophelia. At first Ophelia, a sweet young girl, sang the songs to Hamlet, a cynical actor trying to deliver a speech to the audience. The result was only confusing because there was no reason, explicit or implicit in the text, for Ophelia to address Hamlet. It was more coherent for Ophelia to sing directly to the audience, as if this were her number, and for Hamlet to attempt to interrupt. Hamlet was given various sets of lines, including some of Laertes' heartfelt reactions to the sight of his mad sister, but no set of lines seemed to offer Hamlet sufficient material to compete with Ophelia.

The solution to this problem was found in the work on other scenes. The gravedigger scene (now Scene XXXI) was at first a scene between Hamlet and a mysterious figure who was on stage during the whole performance, playing guitar accompaniment when it was required, subtly influencing the action, and eventually gunning down all the characters in the play at the end. This character was quickly dropped, and all the lines in this scene were given to a trio of old comics (Polonius, Osric, and the Ghost) as a separate stand-up comedy act. (The idea of separate acts or skits had begun when Ophelia's songs began to merge into a "number" which Hamlet interrupted.) The trio of comics was irrelevant, however, and was reduced to one comic, the Ghost, and Hamlet. The rationale for the Ghost's presence was that Hamlet is using the Ghost's grave to bury Ophelia. The idea that Hamlet is burying Ophelia offered a partial solution to both Ophelia's number and the gravedigger scene, because it gave Hamlet a rationale for being in the Ophelia scene (he is there to bury her, an interesting literary point) and it gave the Ghost and Hamlet a situation in which to play the gravedigger scene (Hamlet is the gravedigger, another interesting literary point). Hamlet was therefore given the gravedigger's lines, and the Ghost given Hamlet's lines. The reassigning of lines also gave Hamlet the initiative in the scene and created the idea, which is a literary twist, that Hamlet is a man of the people.

A third current joined the progress of the scene at this point. In the classical text, Hamlet goes to England and disappears from the play for almost five hundred lines. When he returns, his madness appears to have taken a new form. The first attack on this interesting discontinuity in text was to make Hamlet the master of a hundred disguises, a magician who continues to influence the play even though he is apparently no longer there. The one disguise which still remains in this text is Ramon, the Puerto Rican janitor (Hamlet, the man of the people), who at one point in rehearsals was cleaning up during the last major confrontation between Laertes and Claudius until he revealed himself ("This is I, Hamlet the Dane") and joined the duel.

The idea of Ramon cleaning up around the place was joined with the idea of Hamlet burying Ophelia, and Ramon came on with his trash basket and cleaned up Ophelia after he had helped her shoot herself. There was no longer any point to his having lines during her number, which had become more coherent, was arranged for rock music, and had come to include a chorus of guards.

The evolution of these scenes continued in succeeding productions. When Cleavon Little, a Negro, took over as Hamlet, Ramon became Rastus, among many other changes, and the Ghost was replaced by Claudius in the gravedigger scene. Claudius was a cop harassing a poor Negro janitor whose trash basket seemed to be a grave.

The weaving process can be followed until it includes every line and piece of business in the text, and it has been necessary here to exclude arbitrarily many interesting twists and turns which the evolution took, and also the influence of the changes in these scenes on the rest of the play. You will, however, notice many of the echoes as you read the following pages.

HAMLET

by

WILLIAM SHAKESPEARE

as arranged and presented by
The New York Shakespeare Festival
Public Theater

Directed by JOSEPH PAPP

Assisted by TED CORNELL

New York Shakespeare Festival

PUBLIC THEATER

Produced by
JOSEPH PAPP

Artistic Director
GERALD FREEDMAN

Associate Producer
BERNARD GERSTEN

presents
WILLIAM SHAKESPEARE'S

HAMLET

Directed by
JOSEPH PAPP

Scenery by
DAVID MITCHELL

Costumes by
THEONI V. ALDREDGE

Lighting by
MARTIN ARONSTEIN

Music by
GALT MacDERMOT

Musical Director
JOHN MORRIS

with

**JOHN CALL   ANITA DANGLER   JEFF DAVID
MERWIN GOLDSMITH   MICHAEL HEIT
ALBERT QUINTON   APRIL SHAWHAN   MARTIN SHEEN
JAMES J. SLOYAN   RALPH WAITE   FRED WARRINER**

and
**Paul Benjamin   Gerry Black
Paul M. Glaser   Jared Martin   Tom McCready
Paul Speyser   Lisle Wilson**

Ophelia's Act Choreographed by **GEORGE** and **ETHEL MARTIN**

Assistant Director **TED CORNELL**

CAST In Order of Speaking

First Production in the Florence Sutro Anspacher Theater
at the New York Shakespeare Festival
Public Theater

HAMLET	*Martin Sheen*
HORATIO	*Michael Heit*
CLAUDIUS	*Ralph Waite*
OSRIC	*Albert Quinton*
LAERTES	*Jeff David*
POLONIUS	*John Call*
GERTRUDE	*Anita Dangler*
GHOST	*Fred Warriner*
OPHELIA	*April Shawhan*
ROSSENCRAFT	*Merwin Goldsmith*
GILDERSTONE	*James J. Sloyan*
NORWEGIAN CAPTAIN	*Jared Martin*
GUARDS	*Paul Benjamin, Gerry Black, Paul M. Glaser, Jared Martin, Tom McCready, Paul Speyser, Lisle Wilson*

PREFACE: The Guessing Game

Your production starts when the audience enters the theater. The audience tries to figure out from the program, the set, and whatever other evidence is available just what kind of a Hamlet *they are going to see.*

THE FIRST GUESS

As the audience arrives, they see on stage a large, high room, perhaps a prison, perhaps a fortress. The walls, the floor, everything is of gray, unpainted metal. There are two levels of catwalks, one twelve feet above the stage, one at twenty-four feet. Ladders connect the two levels, and at stage right a circular staircase leads from the first level to the stage. In the back wall at stage level are large sliding doors and, higher up, grated windows let in streaks of light. Large metal boxes containing harsh white down lights hang from the forty-foot ceiling. From one of two steel columns supporting the catwalks hangs a white linen suit, double-breasted with a black armband.

"Is it going to be a modern-dress *Hamlet* emphasizing the severe military dictatorship that Claudius has ruthlessly imposed? Is Hamlet the sensitive, young, revolutionary poet?"

THE SECOND GUESS

Some of the audience will read the program. They will see two unfamiliar names: Rossencraft *and* Gilderstone.

"Must be Rosencrantz and Guildenstern, but why fool with the names?"*

They will perhaps read the director's program note which in our case spoke of "gamma-ray shadowgraphing" the play to detect the real Hamlet *beneath the layers of nineteenth-century lacquer. It also spoke of the "shattered focus" of the play, and sought to align our method with the shattering of focus in modern music and painting.*

"Is this *Hamlet* going to be an intellectual fiasco in which nobody knows what is happening and we have to guess our way through it like a T.S. Eliot poem?"

The Third Guess

When the audience is seated, the houselights slowly go out, leaving only moonlight on the empty stage. Suddenly there is a burst of rock music which continues for almost a minute. There is no movement on the stage.

"Is this going to be a rock *Hamlet?* But why is the set like a prison? And what is a rock *Hamlet* anyway?"

(You will probably get a little laugh from the audience at this point, which means they are still guessing.)

> Rehearsal note: The set is like a prison because, when rehearsals began, we thought of Denmark as a prison. We thought of Claudius as having just staged a military coup in the manner of certain modern Latin American or Mediterranean countries. Because it was a time of unrest, the palace or government house was sealed off in the face of street demonstrations. Hamlet was under house arrest because he was the rightful heir to the deposed King and was "loved of the distracted multitude."
>
> During rehearsal, our conception of the play changed and

* *Answer* (not available to the audience): Use these names so no one will take anything for granted, even the text. These names are from the *1603 Quarto*, often called "the corrupt quarto," but remember that any text you read is an amalgam of folios, quartos, and scholarly speculations. There is no extant, crystalline, "original" *Hamlet*.

came to demand rock music. The character of Hamlet's mind —as it developed in Martin Sheen—became more important than the external political situation and began to shape the play in its own way.

We found both a stark prison and rock music in the play, so we put them both in the production. Why restrict yourself to one or the other? Don't make your production any poorer than the original just because you want to seem consistent. You will look like a pauper next to Shakespeare in any case.

THE FOURTH GUESS

At this point, with the rock music still filling the auditorium, you offer the audience a few concrete facts and invite them to assemble their idea of what the court is like. These facts should be thrown on stage very rapidly to convey a sense of urgency and unrest.

One: The sliding doors are thrown open and some guards enter hurriedly pushing the Royal Bed on which GERTRUDE *and* CLAUDIUS *are sleeping.*

Two: Two more guards rush on from the down-right tunnel rolling a plain wooden coffin which they leave at the foot of the Royal Bed. HAMLET *is in the coffin, reading.*

Three: The guards rush into the audience with their flashlights on, looking for anyone suspicious.

Four: One guard—tall, strong, and black—prowls the stage smoking the stub of a cigar. He is Claudius' bodyguard, and at this moment he is carrying Claudius' clothes.

Five: Another guard climbs to the top level of catwalks and slowly scans the audience with his flashlight.

It may not be exactly these facts that any given member of the audience picks up. Other material available to them: The guards wear olive-drab fatigues and combat helmets, black paratroop boots, and one-way mirrored sunglasses. They are armed with .45-caliber automatic pistols and nightsticks. Hamlet is wearing only his underwear, glasses, a beret, and handcuffs. His coffin is fitted like a bed, with mattress and sheets tucked in it. There is also a portable radio in the coffin. The Royal Bed itself is made up with sheets and a blanket; it has two built-in night tables, each with Danish-modern tubular night lights.

Out of these facts the audience may fashion any number of guesses.

"It is a modern dress *Hamlet?* Look at those guards."

"See the bed? That's a symbol. It's going to be an intellectual fiasco."

"Maybe it's a spoof. Why is Hamlet in his underwear? Is that Hamlet?"

> *A word of advice*: This guessing game is essential to your production and will continue with the audience asking themselves about all the devices and situations you offer them. Keep all your choices specific, never vague. If you have two ideas about something, use them both; make both ideas clear, and let the audience choose. Also, never let one idea or device go on too long or it will wear out and the audience will get ahead of you.

Now that you have the audience guessing and open to what you want to tell them, you can begin focusing their attention on the basic conflict of the play. You show them a picture: Hamlet, a little boy, awake in the middle of the night, surrounded by people who are hostile or indifferent toward him. The rock music gives way to the tolling of bells.

SCENE I: By Way of a Prologue

THE FIRST STATEMENT (*military*)

The guards challenge each other across the auditorium, shining their flashlights on whomever is speaking. Hamlet has a flashlight too, and he tries to pick out the various guards with it.

GUARD #1: Who's there?
GUARD #2: Nay, answer me. Stand and unfold yourself.
GUARD #3: Long live the king!
GUARD #4: Bernardo?
GUARD #3: He.

THE SECOND STATEMENT (*civilian*)

Hamlet settles down to his reading and, because he is cold, pulls the blanket off the Royal Bed to cover himself. (Laugh.) Claudius, in his sleep, groans and tries to retrieve the blanket. (Laugh.) A little tug of war starts, as Claudius begins to wake up. (Laugh.)

> *Note*: These laughs are important to you because they get the audience to commit themselves to what they are seeing.

Suddenly there is a commotion and two guards throw a figure in prison stripes and handcuffs on stage from the down-left tunnel. It is HORATIO. *Claudius leaps out of bed with a yell and the bodyguard moves forward with his hand on his gun. Claudius sees who it is and motions the guard away. Horatio sits on the floor next to Hamlet's coffin, as Claudius begins dressing upstage. The bells stop tolling.*

THE THIRD STATEMENT (*personal*)

In this simple scene, the two friends talk, and the audience learns a little about what has happened. Two guards standing in the aisles keep a close eye on the scene. Keep the lights dim; it is still the middle of the night and the court is not yet awake.

HORATIO: My lord Hamlet.

HAMLET [*shaking hands*]: Horatio, my good friend. I am very glad to see you. But what make you from Wittenberg?

HORATIO [*showing handcuffs*]: A truant disposition, my lord.

HAMLET [*sticks out his tongue at a guard*]: I would not hear your enemy say so.

HORATIO: My lord, I came to see your father's funeral.

HAMLET: I prithee, do not mock me, fellow-student. I think it was to see my mother's wedding.

HORATIO: Indeed, it followed hard upon.

HAMLET: Thrift, thrift, Horatio! the funeral baked meats did coldly furnish forth the marriage tables. Would that I had met my dearest foe in heaven or ever I had seen that day, Horatio.

> *Note*: A simple scene is good, but it must not go on too long. You should introduce a series of twists.

THE FIRST TWIST

A photograph portrait of Hamlet's father lights up on the back wall. Only Hamlet sees it. By showing the picture, you make absolutely clear why Hamlet says the line, even though there is no explanation for the picture.

HAMLET: MY FATHER! METHINKS I SEE MY FATHER!

HORATIO: Where, my lord?

The photograph disappears.

HAMLET: In my mind's eye, Horatio.

HORATIO: I saw him once; he was a goodly king.

HAMLET: He was a man! take him for all in all. I shall not look upon his like again.

THE SECOND TWIST

Here you let the audience know that you are not only doing Hamlet, *but you are also doing a play about* Hamlet. *Underplay this.*

HORATIO: What do you read, my lord?

HAMLET: *Hamlet*, an excellent play, well digested in the scenes, set down with as much modesty as cunning. I remember one said there were no sallets in the lines to make the matter more savoury, nor no matter in the phrase that might indict the author of affectation, but called it an honest work, as wholesome as sweet and by very much more handsome than fine.

HORATIO: 'Tis caviar to the general.

HAMLET: He's for a jig or a tale of bawdry or he sleeps. [*He reads from the text.*] So oft it chances in particular men, that for some vicious mole of nature in them, as in their birth—

THE THIRD TWIST

Horatio already knows the play. He quotes from memory the speech Hamlet is reading.

HORATIO: —wherein they are not guilty since nature cannot choose his origin—

HAMLET: By o'ergrowth of some complexion oft breaking down the pales and forts of reason—

HORATIO: Or by some habit that too much o'er-leavens the form of plausive manners—

HAMLET: That these men, carrying, as I say, the stamp of one defect, shall in the general censure take corruption from that particular fault.

THE LAST TWIST

which twists the audience back into the play. Hamlet acknowl-edges that the play is beginning when he hears an alarm clock ringing off stage. The lights begin to brighten and there is a commotion in the wings.

HAMLET: They are coming to the play. We must be idle. Get you a place.

The lights come up full as POLONIUS *enters carrying the ringing alarm clock. He is followed by* LAERTES *and* OPHELIA. OSRIC *also enters, and on the first level catwalk a guard brings on a large photo-portrait of Hamlet's father in military uniform. Gertrude sits up in bed and starts combing her hair. A guard takes Horatio over to one corner of the stage, and Claudius signals Polonius to shut off the clock. Finally everyone is in place. Claudius takes the cigar out of his mouth and looks around.*

> *Style note*: Look what you have done. You have given the audience a nice clear situation: the court assembling in the morning. But the Queen is in bed, and Hamlet is in his coffin. If you have been successful, you have not only established that this is going to be a modern *Hamlet*, but a ridiculous *Hamlet*. If the audience is alert, they will know to expect more than just a modern translation. This is why the Royal Bed is a key to this scene; it is concrete and ridiculous at the same time, hitting the Freudian interpretation over the head.

SCENE II: Claudius Tells Everyone
What Is Happening

A word of advice: Don't make Claudius a villain. Sure, he wears a pistol in his shoulder holster, smokes a cigar, and has a three-day beard. Sure, he has his guards, but at heart he is a nice, simple guy. He can't understand Hamlet and doesn't care about him. When Hamlet attacks him, he will fight back, but for now Hamlet is just an annoyance. Give Hamlet the initiative in this battle, as you will give Hamlet the initiative in the whole play.

CLAUDIUS [*referring to photo-portrait above*]: Though yet of Hamlet our dear brother's death the memory be green, yet so far hath discretion fought with nature that we with wisest sorrow think on him together with remembrance of ourselves. Therefore, our sometime sister, now our queen [*he gives Gertrude a kiss on the neck; she giggles*], have we, as 'twere with a defeated joy, taken to wife. Nor have we herein barr'd your better wisdoms, which have freely gone with this affair along. For all, our thanks. [*Everyone applauds.*]

THE STUPID GUARD BIT

So much for him. Now for ourselves and this time of meeting.

The guard exits with the photograph of Old Hamlet, and a second guard, carrying a portrait of Claudius, takes his place. The picture is upside down. Hamlet and the audience see this and laugh.   —*Joke No. 1*

CLAUDIUS: [*He sees what's wrong, swears, and picks up the phone.*] Paul!   —*Joke No. 2*

GUARD [*looks down and answers*]: Yeah, Ralph.
>   —*Old Joke No. 3, using the actor's real*
>   *name. (It wasn't supposed to happen.)*
>   —*New Joke No. 3A, why talk into*
>   *the phone?*

CLAUDIUS: The damned thing is upside down.
GUARD: Jesus, Ralph, I'm sorry. [*He turns the picture right side up.*]   —*Cheap Joke No. 4, colloquial language*

> *About cheap jokes:* Why stoop to such devices as the use of
> colloquial language and slapstick humor? Perhaps to let a little
> air into the play and make it approachable. Shakespeare's work
> had such moments for its original audience, and we are poorer
> because they are not always as funny for us. Use these collo-
> quial sections as a guide in your work. If every moment in the
> play is not as alive and immediate as these moments, then you
> are not doing your job but simply leaning on Shakespeare's
> reputation.

CLAUDIUS: You know, young Fortinbras, holding a weak supposal
of our worth, or thinking by our late dear brother's death our
state to be disjoint and out of frame, colleagued with this
dream of his advantage. He hath not fail'd to pester us with
message, importing the surrender of those lands lost by his
father with all bands of law to our most valiant brother. Thus
much the business is: [*Polonius hands him a manila envelope*]
we have here writ to Norway, uncle of young Fortinbras,
who, impotent and bed-rid, feigns he hears not of this his
nephew's purpose, to suppress his further gait herein or face
the might of our wrathful armies. [*He gives the envelope to
Osric who comes forward eagerly.*]

The Stupid Messenger Bit (*subtle*)

[*Claudius speaks very slowly and carefully to Osric who, eager to please on his last mission, gave away several provinces without royal authorization.*] And we here dispatch you, good Osric, to bear this demand to old Norway, giving to you no further personal power to business with the king, more than the scope of these delated articles allow. Farewell and let your haste commend your duty.

OSRIC [*always ready*]: In that and all things will I show my duty.

CLAUDIUS [*hand to forehead*]: We doubt it nothing: heartily farewell.

Osric salutes elaborately and exits.

The Interruption Bit

Claudius is reluctant to talk to Hamlet, but gives Laertes a hearty send-off.

CLAUDIUS: Now, my cousin Hamlet . . .

LAERTES: My dread Lord . . .

CLAUDIUS: Laertes, what's the news with you? You told us of some suit, what is't, Laertes?

LAERTES: My dread lord, your leave and favour to return to France, from whence I came to show my duty in your coronation.

CLAUDIUS: Have you your father's leave? What says Polonius?

POLONIUS: He hath, my lord. I do beseech you give him leave to go.

CLAUDIUS: Take thy fair hour, Laertes. Time be thine, and thy best graces spend it at thy will. [*He gives Laertes a slap on the back, as Polonius ushers off his children, and then he turns back to the unpleasant business of talking to Hamlet. He points to Horatio.*] Get him outta here!

A guard hustles Horatio out and Claudius confronts Hamlet wearily.

SCENE III: The Family Talks Things Over

THE STEPFATHER TRIES TO REACH THE BOY

CLAUDIUS: Now, my cousin Hamlet, and my son—
HAMLET: A little more than kin, and less than kind.
CLAUDIUS: How is it that the clouds still hang on you?
HAMLET: Not so, my lord; I am too much in the sun.

Claudius shrugs and moves away. Gertrude gets out of bed and moves coyly to Hamlet, who is still sitting in his coffin.

THE MOTHER TRIES

GERTRUDE: Good Hamlet, cast thy nighted colour off, and let thine eye look like a friend on Denmark. Do not for ever with thy veiled lids seek for thy noble father in the dust. Thou know'st 'tis common, all that live must die, passing through nature to eternity.

CLAUDIUS BACKS HER UP

CLAUDIUS: That's right. [*He is tying his shoe.*]
HAMLET: Ay, madam, it is common.
GERTRUDE: If it be, why seems it so particular with thee?
HAMLET: Seems, madam? Nay, it is. I know not "seems."

Hamlet throws a pillow at his mother who gasps and moves away in a huff. Claudius moves in to quiet things down and make—

THE BIG PITCH

CLAUDIUS: 'Tis sweet and commendable in your nature, Hamlet, to give these mourning duties to your father. But to persevere in obstinate condolement is a course of impious stubbornness. 'Tis unmanly grief.

THE I'M-A-BIG-BOY-NOW BIT

Hamlet clambers out of the coffin, throws out his chest and postures about the stage. Claudius takes a deep breath and tries again.

THE LINE-OF-SUCCESSION PLOY
(*spoken in part to the audience*)

CLAUDIUS: We pray you throw to earth this unprevailing woe, and think of us as of a father. [*To audience*] For let the world take note, he is the most immediate to our throne, and with no less nobility of love than that which dearest father bears his son do I impart toward him.

THE PRISONER BIT

Hamlet throws up his hands and shows the audience his handcuffs.

THE KEY GAMBIT

CLAUDIUS [*takes a key from his pocket and dangles it in front of Hamlet*]: For your intent in going back to school in Wittenberg, it is most retrograde to our desire, and we beseech you, bend you to remain here in the cheer and comfort of our eye, our chiefest courtier, cousin, and our son.

GERTRUDE [*takes the key from Claudius and goes to Hamlet with it*]: Let not thy mother lose her prayers, Hamlet. I pray thee, stay with us. Go not to Wittenberg.

THE KEY GAMBIT WORKS

HAMLET: I shall in all my best obey you, madam.

Gertrude unlocks the handcuffs.

CLAUDIUS: Why, 'tis a loving and a fair reply.
Be as ourself in Denmark.

Gertrude and Claudius go out through the up-center doors. The bodyguard takes Hamlet's clothes off the light switch where they have been hanging and throws them in the coffin. He then shuts out the light and exits with Gertrude and Claudius, closing the sliding doors behind them.

SCENE IV: Hamlet Is Still Alone

He begins to dress, putting on his shirt, tie, and jacket while speaking to the audience.

HAMLET: Fie on't! ah, fie! 'tis an unweeded garden,
That grows to seed; things rank and gross in nature
Possess it merely. That it should come to this!
But two months dead! nay, not so much, not two.
So excellent a king, that was to this
Hyperion to a satyr; so loving to my mother
That he might not beteem the winds of heaven
Visit her face too roughly. Heaven and earth!
Must I remember? Why, she would hang on him,
As if increase of appetite had grown
By what it fed on; and yet, within a month—
Let me not think on't! Frailty, thy name is woman.
A little month, or ere those shoes were old
With which she follow'd my poor father's body,
Like Niobe, all tears; why she, even she—
O God! a beast, that wants discourse of reason,
Would have mourn'd longer—married with my uncle,
My father's brother, but no more like my father
Than I to Hercules. Within a month,
Ere yet the salt of most unrighteous tears
Had left the flushing in her galled eyes,
She married. O most wicked speed, to post
With such dexterity to incestuous sheets.
It is not, nor it cannot come to, good.
But break, my heart, for I must hold my tongue.

The Supernatural Occurrence

Hamlet sits in his coffin-bed, turns on his radio, and begins reading. The radio offers ghostly wailing instead of music and Hamlet tries to adjust it. —*The Set-Up*

A long, green, rubber hand emerges from the bed-clothes and starts to feel its way across the sheets to Hamlet. —*Joke No. 1*

Audience laughs and gasps. Hamlet looks up and asks the audience what is the matter. —*Joke No. 2*

The hand touches Hamlet on the shoulder. He leaps out of his coffin and begins flailing with his pillow at the figure which emerges from the bed-clothes.

HAMLET: Angels and ministers of grace defend us!
—*Joke No. 3, general laughter*

> *Rehearsal note*: The Ghost of Hamlet's father (who is now in the process of appearing) is a key to the production, but was one of the last elements to fall into place. We found ourselves lost in a maze of mechanical devices trying to make the idea of the supernatural real. To most people, however, Ghosts are funny and this is their reality. You must undercut the ponderous seriousness of the Ghost without losing his importance. Stick to the facts: he is Hamlet's father, but he is out of touch, something of an orator, an old-time vaudevillian. Choose an actor with a lot of charm, a sense of humor, and a good Elizabethan voice.

> *Costume note*: The Ghost wears long underwear and a burned-out, battered, camouflaged army helmet. He will put various costumes over this basic outfit.

SCENE V: A Traveler Returns

GHOST: Mark me.
HAMLET: I will.
GHOST: I am thy father's spirit—

THE DUAL-REACTION-AND-AUDIENCE-INVOLVEMENT BIT

Hamlet cheers and runs like a scared rabbit out into the audience. He stays there for some time hiding and cheering.

—doom'd for a certain term to walk the night, and for the day confined to fast in fires, till the foul crimes done in my days of nature are burnt and purg'd away.
HAMLET: Alas, poor ghost!
GHOST: List, list, O, list!

THE GHOST'S-DESPERATE-NEED-TO-COMMUNICATE BIT (PART I)

He sputters and turns off the radio. The ghostly noises cease. (Laugh.) He speaks directly to someone in the audience. (Laugh.)

> *Helpful hint*: If the actor playing the Ghost asks why he should address someone in the audience at this point, your readiest answer is, of course, "Why not?" If you want to elaborate, point out that the audience is there just as much as Hamlet is, that each of them has a father, and that it is just as important for them to know what is happening as it is for Hamlet.

GHOST: If thou didst ever thy dear father love—

HAMLET: O God!

GHOST: Revenge his foul and most unnatural murder.

HAMLET: Murder?

GHOST: Murder most foul, as in the best it is, but this most foul, strange and unnatural.

HAMLET: Haste me to know't, that I may sweep to my revenge.

GHOST: Now, Hamlet, hear. 'Tis given out, that sleeping in my orchard the lightning struck me.

THE GHOST'S-DESPERATE-NEED-TO-COMMUNICATE BIT (PART II)

The Ghost produces a newspaper with the banner headline: KING STRUCK BY LIGHTNING. *(Huge laugh.)*

THE GHOST'S-DESPERATE-NEED-TO-COMMUNICATE BIT (PART III)

Hamlet takes the opportunity to run back on stage and start climbing up the circular staircase to the catwalks. The Ghost pursues him, throwing down the paper.

GHOST: But know, thou noble youth, the lightning that did burn thy father's flesh now wears his crown.

HAMLET: O my prophetic soul. My uncle?

GHOST: Ay, that incestuous, that adulterate beast won to his shameful lust the will of my most seeming-virtuous queen.

HAMLET: O horrible! O horrible!

The Ghost's-Desperate-Need-to-Communicate (or Do Something) Bit (Part IV)

Hamlet, who has reached the very top level of catwalks, lets down a rope swing. The Ghost, who is on his way up a ladder in pursuit of Hamlet, grabs the rope swing and puts one foot in it, balancing precariously between the ladder and the swing. (Growing laughter.) The Ghost swings, talking all the while.

GHOST: If thou hast nature in thee, bear it not. Let not the royal bed of Denmark be a couch for luxury and damned incest. But, howsoever thou pursuest this act, taint not thy mind, nor let thy soul contrive against thy mother aught. Leave her to heaven, and to those thorns that in her bosom lodge to prick and sting her.

The Ghost's Farewell

The ghostly wailing resumes. The Ghost stops swinging abruptly and murmurs, "Uh oh!" (Huge laugh.) He gets off the swing and begins to exit, bowing to the audience with each "Adieu!"

GHOST: Fare thee well at once! Adieu, adieu, adieu. [*He makes a false exit and returns immediately for a last triumphant*] Remember me! [*He exits to applause and cheers which are led by Hamlet.*]

> Note: The audience will applaud and cheer three times out of four if the actor playing the Ghost is doing his job. If they don't applaud, Hamlet's own reaction is sufficient.

Hamlet Addresses the Multitude

Hamlet, still on the top level, picks up a microphone and speaks over the public address system.

HAMLET: Remember thee? Ay, thou poor ghost, while memory holds a seat in this distracted globe. Remember thee? Yes, from the table of my memory I'll wipe away all trivial fond records, and thy commandments all alone shall live within the book and volume of my brain, unmix'd with baser matter.

HAMLET SWINGS INTO ACTION

He puts down the microphone and begins to climb down to the stage floor very rapidly.

> *Note*: What you must have created by this point is a tremendous sense of excitement. A change has come over Hamlet; he is no longer the little boy of the first scenes.

HAMLET: Yes, by heaven! O most pernicious woman! O villain, villain, smiling, damned villain! That one may smile, and smile, and be a villain!

SCENE VI: The Two Friends Meet Again But Hamlet Has Changed

THE WHAT-ARE-YOU-TALKING-ABOUT BIT

Horatio is excited because he has escaped. He comes running on with the handcuffs dangling from one wrist. Hamlet is excited for obvious reasons. He jumps from the circular staircase, throws a headlock on Horatio, and wrestles him to the ground. He then gets up and starts arranging his coffin, pointing it toward the down-right tunnel.

HORATIO: My lord, my lord! How is it, my noble lord?

HAMLET: News, Horatio.

HORATIO: What news, my lord?

HAMLET: O wonderful!

HORATIO: Good my lord, tell it.

HAMLET: No; you will reveal it.

HORATIO: Not I, my lord, by heaven!

HAMLET: How say you, then? Would heart of man once think it? But you'll be secret?

HORATIO: By heaven, my lord.

HAMLET: An apparition appeared before me with this message [*He shows Horatio the newspaper headline*].

HORATIO: What message, my lord?

HAMLET [*pointing to headline*]: There's ne'er a villain dwelling in all Denmark, but he's an arrant knave.

HORATIO: There needs no ghost to tell us this.

The Go-Away-Boy-You-Bother-Me Bit

Hamlet pockets the newspaper, shakes hands with Horatio, and shoves him toward an exit. He then rapidly puts on his pants and finishes dressing.

HAMLET: Why right; you are in the right; and so, without more circumstance at all, I hold it fit that we shake hands and part; you, as your business and desire shall point you—for every man hath business and desire, such as it is—and, for my own poor part, I will go pray.

HORATIO: These are but wild and whirling words, my lord.

HAMLET: I am sorry they offend you, heartily; yes, 'faith, heartily.

HORATIO: There's no offence, my lord.

HAMLET [*shouting*]: Yes, by Saint Patrick, but there is, Horatio, and much offence, too.

The "Old Mole" Returns (*in part*)

Hamlet is jubilant, Horatio amazed.

GHOST [*offstage*]: Hamlet!

HAMLET: Ha, ha, boy! say'st thou so? [*To Horatio*] Canst hear this fellow?

HORATIO: But this is wondrous strange.

HAMLET: There are more things in heaven and earth, Horatio, than are dreamt of in your philosophy.

The Old Mole Returns (*all of him*)

GHOST [*dances swiftly across the stage*]: Remember me!

HAMLET: Rest, rest, perturbed spirit.

Note: There are many ways to have the Ghost return. He can throw a newspaper at Hamlet from the catwalk, or he can hit him with his rubber glove. Try them all and leave it up to the Ghost.

THE RECAPTURE OF HORATIO

Two guards run on suddenly and grab Horatio. They hustle him off stage. Hamlet is too busy to notice because he has heard some-one and seems to be making some sort of preparations for the next scene.

HORATIO: Good night, my lord.
HAMLET: Good night, Horatio.

He aims his coffin so it is pointing down one of the tunnels, dims the lights, and turns on his radio so it is playing soft music. He runs a little way into the audience to hide, and Polonius jovially ushers in his children.

SCENE VII: A Few Precepts

THE HAPPY FAMILY TABLEAU

Polonius and Laertes clink champagne glasses in a cheerful toast, and Ophelia leans against the circular staircase to listen to her father. Polonius moves down stage to address the audience, and Laertes offers Ophelia a sip of champagne. As Polonius continues talking in this position, Laertes begins mocking him behind his back. Meanwhile, there is also in progress . . .

THE ILLICIT ASSIGNATION BIT

Hamlet from the audience is shining his flashlight on Ophelia's face. She is aware of this and is obviously delighted.

POLONIUS: And these few precepts in thy memory look thou character. Be thou familiar, but by no means vulgar; beware of entrance to a quarrel, but, being in, bear it that the opposed may beware of thee. Give every man thy ear, but few thy voice. Take each man's censure, but reserve thy judgement. Costly thy habit as thy purse can buy, but not expressed in fancy; rich, not gaudy; for the apparel oft proclaims the man. Neither a borrower, nor a lender be. For loan oft loses both itself and friend, and borrowing dulls the edge of husbandry.

The Fateful Exit

[*Polonius turns to his son and throws an arm around his shoulders. He speaks his last line as they exit out the tunnel.*] This above all: to thine own self be true. And it must follow, as the night the day, thou canst not then be false to any man.

Ophelia lingers behind, and Hamlet sneaks on stage.

SCENE VIII: The Shortest Scene
in the Play

HAMLET: Ophelia!

OPHELIA: Oh Hamlet!

Hamlet picks up Ophelia and puts her in his coffin. She lies down; he turns out the lights and places his flashlight in the coffin so that it shines on her face. The soft music is still playing.

HAMLET: Nymph, in thy orisons be all my sins remembered.

He laughs, she giggles, and he rolls his coffin and his prize out the tunnel.

SCENE IX: Polonius Lays Down the Law

THE TERRIBLE DISCOVERY BIT

Polonius enters the darkened stage, carrying a flashlight which he shines around the stage and audience.

POLONIUS: Ophelia? Ophelia?   —*First Laugh*

He shines the flashlight down the tunnel where Hamlet and Ophelia exited.

OPHELIA!   —*Second Laugh*

There is the sound of running footsteps. Polonius goes to the light switch and snaps on the lights. Ophelia is revealed, wearing only her slip and carrying her shoes.   —*Third Laugh*

THE FATHER GIVES HIS DAUGHTER
ENOUGH ROPE TO HANG HERSELF

Polonius stands and listens quietly, offering occasional comments as Ophelia tries to talk her way out of her predicament. She puts on her shoes and moves about the stage as she talks, occasionally getting caught up in the story she is inventing.

POLONIUS: How now, Ophelia! What's the matter?
OPHELIA: O, my lord, my lord, I have been so affrighted!
POLONIUS: With what, i' the name of God?
OPHELIA: My lord, as I was sewing in my closet, Lord Hamlet, with his doublet all unbrac'd, pale as his shirt, his knees knocking each other, and with a look so piteous in purport as if he had been loosed out of hell to speak of horrors—he comes before me.

POLONIUS: Conceit upon his father?

OPHELIA: My lord, I do not know, but truly I do fear it.

POLONIUS: What said he?

OPHELIA: He took me by the wrist and held me hard. Then goes he to the length of all his arm and with his other hand thus o'er his brow, he falls to such perusal of my face as he would draw it. That done, he lets me go, and with his head over his shoulder turn'd he seem'd to find his way without his eyes. For out o' doors he went without their helps, and to the last bended their light on me.

POLONIUS: What, have you given him any hard words of late?

OPHELIA: No, my good lord.

POLONIUS TIGHTENS THE NOOSE, BUT OPHELIA ESCAPES

POLONIUS [*produces a packet of letters tied with a pink bow*]: What is between you? Give me up the truth.

OPHELIA: He hath, my lord, of late made many tenders of his affection to me. [*She grabs the letters and runs away.*]

THE MERRY CHASE

Polonius chases Ophelia as she dodges in and out of the columns and around the circular staircase.

POLONIUS [*chasing her*]: Affection? Pooh! You speak like a green girl unsifted in such perilous circumstance. Do you believe his tenders, as you call them?

OPHELIA [*evading him*]: I do not know, my lord, what I should think.

POLONIUS: Marry, I will teach you. [*He catches her and gives her a spank. She squeals and runs into the audience.*] Think yourself a baby that you have taken these tenders for true pay.

OPHELIA: My lord, he hath before importuned me with love in honorable fashion.

POLONIUS [*exhausted, he stops, out of breath, in the middle of the stage to lecture his wayward daughter*]: Ay, fashion you may call it. Go to, go to. Springes to catch woodcocks. I do know when the blood burns, how prodigal the soul lends the tongue vows. This is for all: I would not, in plain terms, from this time forth have you so slander any moment's leisure as to give words or talk with the lord Hamlet.

> *Style note*: Do not play this scene for laughs. The audience will, of course, laugh when they see a little fat old man running around trying to give his daughter a spanking, but Polonius himself must be serious about his business. There is a very effective and pathetic point to be made when Polonius stops, completely out of breath, and tries to tell his daughter what is on his mind. Remember that Hamlet makes the jokes; it is he who will turn the play and the characters in it upside down. The other characters must let Hamlet play the jokes on them. If they are funny they must not know it, or give any indication that they want to be; otherwise they will take away Hamlet's trump card.

HAMLET INTERRUPTS THE PLAY

HAMLET [*appears at the back of the house and calls out*]:

INTERMISSION! HOUSELIGHTS!

The houselights do in fact come on, and Hamlet immediately exits. Polonius now has a hard time keeping Ophelia's attention because she runs across the stage to see what Hamlet is up to. He succeeds, however, in giving her his last instructions and goes to hide behind the circular staircase. She is still impudent.

POLONIUS: Here he comes. Ophelia, mark me and do as I command. Return you these his letters and deny his access to you. Look to't, I charge you.

SCENE X: The Peanut Scene

Rehearsal note: This is a crucial scene in this production, and it was one of the last to fall into place in rehearsal. The problem is to give life to Hamlet's new-found antic disposition in a production that is already antic at its very core. The solution is to have Hamlet abandon the form of the play altogether and work directly with the audience. He denies even that he is Hamlet and becomes a peanut vendor.

THE BASIC PEANUT VENDOR BIT

Hamlet enters at the back of the house wearing a straw hat, carrying several helium-filled balloons on strings and a vendor's tray filled with bags of peanuts. He moves down one aisle calling out:

PEANUTS AND BALLOONS! GET YOUR PEANUTS!

and other suitable phrases. Someone will offer him a quarter, and he says:

Sorry, no change. GET YOUR PEANUTS AND BALLOONS!

He may give out a few bags of peanuts, and he also holds out a balloon to a woman in the audience. She reaches for it, but he lets go and it floats up to the ceiling of the theater. Of course all this activity is improvised and changes with each new audience. It successfully interrupts the play, and now Ophelia must attract Hamlet's and the audience's attention. She holds out the packet of letters.

OPHELIA: My lord, I have remembrances of yours that I have longed long to re-deliver. I pray you now receive them.

HAMLET [*notices the little girl who is bothering him, takes the packet of letters, looks at it, smiles, and throws it back on stage*]: No, not I. I never gave you aught.

OPHELIA [*retrieves the packet and again holds it out to Hamlet, who is still busy selling peanuts and balloons*]: My honour'd lord, you know right well you did, and with them words of so sweet breath compos'd as made the things more rich. Their perfume lost, take these again, for to the noble mind rich gifts wax poor when givers prove unkind. There, my lord.

The First Variation on the Basic Peanut Vendor Bit

Hamlet realizes that he is going to have to deal with this little girl and he asks some member of the audience to hold the balloons while he goes on stage and gives her a good talking to. He then has second thoughts about letting someone hold the balloons, and he questions the man.

HAMLET: Are you honest?

OPHELIA [*wants to know what Hamlet is up to*]: My lord?

HAMLET [*to man in audience*]: Are you fair?

OPHELIA: What means your lordship?

HAMLET [*to man or woman in audience*]: That if you be honest and fair, your honesty should admit no discourse to your beauty. [*He takes back the balloons and moves up the aisle, continuing to hawk his peanuts.*]

OPHELIA: Could beauty, my lord, have better commerce than with honesty?

HAMLET [*to Ophelia*]: Ay, truly; for the power of beauty will sooner transform honesty from what it is to a bawd than the force of honesty can translate beauty into his likeness. This was sometime a paradox, but now the time gives it proof.

The Second Variation

HAMLET [*gives a girl in the audience a balloon and says to her*]:
I did love you once.

OPHELIA: Indeed, my lord, you made me believe so.

HAMLET: You should not have believed me, for virtue cannot so
innoculate our old stock but we shall relish of it. I loved you
not. [*He snatches back the balloon, and again moves into the
audience.*]

OPHELIA: I was the more deceived.

The Third Variation

HAMLET [*shows a trace of annoyance with this little girl who
will not let him alone. He throws a bag of peanuts at her.*]:
Get thee to a nunnery. Why wouldst thou be a breeder of
sinners? [*He explains himself to the audience, or, perhaps,
singles out one individual and sits next to him.*] I am myself
indifferent honest, but yet I could accuse me of such things
that it were better my mother had not borne me. I am very
proud, revengeful, ambitious, with more offences at my beck
than I have thoughts to put them in, imagination to give them
shape, or time to act them in. What should such fellows as I
do crawling between earth and heaven?

The Discovery of Polonius

HAMLET [*gets up and moves rapidly to the stage. To man in
audience*]: We are arrant knaves all; believe none of us. Go
thy ways to a nunnery. Where's your father?

OPHELIA: At home, my lord.

HAMLET [*moves quickly past Ophelia and around the circular*

staircase, giving Polonius a kick in the pants as he goes past]:
Let the doors be shut upon him, that he may play the fool no
where but in's own house.

OPHELIA: O, help him, you sweet heavens!

THE FOURTH VARIATION

HAMLET [*offers a balloon to a lady in the first row on one condition*]: If thou dost marry, I'll give thee this plague for thy
dowry. Be thou as chaste as ice, as pure as snow, thou shalt
not escape calumny. [*He gives her the balloon and shakes
hands with her husband or escort.*] Marry a fool, for wise men
know well enough what monsters you make of them.

OPHELIA: Heavenly powers, restore him!

THE FIFTH AND FINAL VARIATION ON THE PEANUT VENDOR BIT

*Hamlet throws a hail of peanut bags at Ophelia. Polonius tries in
vain to shield his daughter from this madman, but Hamlet drives
her off the stage in tears, throwing peanuts at her even as she
escapes down the tunnel.*

HAMLET: The rest shall keep as they are. To a nunnery, go. And
quickly too. Farewell! I have heard of your paintings well
enough. God hath given you one face, and you make your-
selves another. You fig and amble and you lisp. You nickname
God's creatures, and make your wantonness your ignorance.
Go to, I'll no more on't. It hath made me mad. I say we will
have no more marriages. Those that are married already, all
but one, shall live.

SCENE XI: The Peanut Scene Reprise

The Identification Bit

Polonius speaks harshly to Hamlet, but Hamlet is in good spirits once again. He gives the old man a hearty handshake.

POLONIUS: How does my good Lord Hamlet?
HAMLET [*jovial*]: Well, God-a-mercy.
POLONIUS: Do you know me, my lord?
HAMLET: Excellent well. You are a fishmonger.
POLONIUS: Not I, my lord.
HAMLET: Have you a daughter?
POLONIUS: I have, my lord.
HAMLET: Let her not walk i' the sun. Conception is a blessing; but as your daughter may conceive—friend, look to't. [*He puts the strap of the vendor's tray around Polonius' neck, and then sits in the audience, leaving the old man with the peanuts.*]

The Reading Matter Bit

POLONIUS [*getting more and more confused*]: How say you by that? Yet he knew me not at first. He said I was a fishmonger. He is far gone, far gone. What do you read, my lord?
HAMLET: The program.

> *Note*: There are many alternatives you might want to use here. When Cleavon Little, a Negro, was playing Hamlet, he was reading *Ebony*. After our scathing review in *The New York Times*, Hamlet was reading that newspaper for a while. Use a local publication.

POLONIUS: What is the matter, my lord?

HAMLET [*stands up, looking for a fight*]: Between who?

POLONIUS: I mean the matter that you read, my lord.

HAMLET [*sits down and reads from whatever it is he is reading*]:
Slanders, sir! For the satirical rogue says here that old men
have grey beards, that their faces are wrinkled, their eyes
purging thick amber and plum-tree gum, and that they have
a plentiful lack of wit, together with most weak hams.

POLONIUS: Though this be madness, yet there is method in't. My
honorable lord, I will most humbly take my leave of you.

HAMLET [*already on his way out, having crossed the stage and
climbed the circular staircase to the first level*]: You cannot
take from me anything that I will not more willingly part
withal—except my life, except my life, except my life.

> *Note*: An alternate to this line which was often used is:
> "Except my wife. Except my *wife*? Except my *life*!" This line
> provides a suitably large laugh to end the sequence on a high
> note. If your sense of taste prevents you from treating the
> text so callously, simply have Hamlet throw one last bag of
> peanuts at Polonius.

*Hamlet exits cheerfully above, and Polonius exits out one of the
tunnels, muttering to himself.*

> *Scholarly query*: "Is Hamlet mad or only pretending to be
> mad?" This question has vexed scholars for generations, and
> the answer can now be seen clearly to be, "No." If an actor
> and not a scholar asks this question, tell him to play the scene
> that is put before him and not to concern himself or the
> audience with psychology.

SCENE XII: Claudius and Gertrude Welcome Two Old Friends of Hamlet to the Palace

Style note: Hamlet has been breaking up the play, but now the plot resumes. To re-establish the context of the play, have the lights go out at the close of the last scene, allow a brief pause, and then have the guards throw open the center doors as they did at the opening of the play. The lights then come up and ROSSENCRAFT and GILDERSTONE, two college students dressed in blazers and slacks, wander on stage through the doors. This device will reassert the structure of the play and allow Hamlet once again to break it open.

THE CLAUDIUS-IS-A-LITTLE-LATE BIT

Gertrude enters through the center doors and turns around to motion for Claudius. He enters reading a newspaper and muttering.

CLAUDIUS: All right, all right. [*He still isn't overly concerned about Hamlet's activities, apparently. He folds the newspaper and moves to shake hands with Rossencraft.*]

THE OH-ARE-THERE-TWO-OF-THEM BIT

Welcome dear Rossencraft, moreover that we much did—
GERTRUDE: Claudius? [*She points to Gilderstone, who is standing on the other side of the stage, and smiles sweetly, trying to make everything go smoothly.*]

CLAUDIUS: Who's that?

GERTRUDE: Gilderstone.

CLAUDIUS: Oh, welcome dear Gilderstone. [*He shakes his hand and then launches into his speech.*]

CLAUDIUS' PLAN

Moreover that we much did long to see you, the need we have to use you did provoke our hasty sending. Something have you heard of Hamlet's transformation. So I call it, since nor th' exterior nor the inward man resembles that it was. What it should be, more than his father's death, that thus hath put him so much from the understanding of himself, I cannot dream of. I entreat you both, that being of so young days brought up with him, and since so neighbour'd to his youth and haviour, that you vouchsafe your rest here in our court some little time; so by your companies to draw him on to pleasures and to gather, so much as from occasion you may glean, whether aught to us unknown afflicts him thus, that, open'd, lies within our remedy.

Claudius, having finished making his pitch to Rossencraft and Gilderstone, moves up stage to read his newspaper while Gertrude speaks to the two boys. As she is speaking, the following routine begins.

THE RAMON ROUTINE (PART I)

Hamlet enters disguised as the porter Ramon, wearing a peeling leather jacket, baggy pants, combination false nose and glasses, and a paste-on moustache. He hums a pleasing little Spanish tune.

—*First Joke*

He sets down the garbage can he is carrying and begins to sweep up with a long-handled broom which he moves in and around the legs of Claudius, Gertrude, Rossencraft, and Gilderstone. Although he is annoying, he doesn't really exist to the others, and they ignore him. —*Second Joke*

He cleans up the left-over peanut bags from the previous scene and then picks up the discarded love letters from the previous scene. But they are only a curiosity to the janitor and he tosses them into the trash basket. —*Third Joke, sad*

GERTRUDE: Good gentlemen, he hath much talked of you; and sure I am two men there are not living to whom he more adheres. If it will please you to show us so much gentry and good will as to expend your time with us awhile, for the supply and profit of our hope, your visitation shall receive such thanks as fits a king's remembrance.

THE RAMON ROUTINE (PART II)

The King-is-always-broke bit. Gertrude notices that Claudius hasn't been listening, so she cues him to give the boys a little money.

GERTRUDE: Claudius? As fits a king's remembrance?
—*First Joke, contemporary comment on Shakespeare's line*

Claudius chuckles and fishes around in his pockets for some cash. He is a little embarrassed at being broke.
—*Second Joke, contemporary behavioral comment that the rich never have any cash*

CLAUDIUS [*turns to a tough wiry guard at the door*]: Rachel, you got any money?
—*Third Joke, cheap use of a girl's name for the tough guard, also some nervous laughter over the use of such crass language*

Rachel turns his pockets out and points to Claudius' bodyguard who is also standing by the door.

Alice, could you lend me a couple of bucks?

—Third Joke continues

Alice shakes his head no and points to Ramon. The language barrier bit.

Hey, Ramon, you got a couple of dollars you could—

RAMON: Que? *—Fourth Joke*

RACHEL [*explains to Ramon what is wanted. He points at Claudius and yells*]: Dineros, dineros!
RAMON: Ah, si, si, si. *—Fifth Joke*

The fantastically wealthy janitor bit. Ramon takes a huge wad of bills out of his pocket. *—Sixth Joke*

He sees that everyone is looking at him and he tries to hide the wad. He peels off two bills and gives them to Claudius.

—Seventh Joke, old world suspicion

CLAUDIUS: Thank you very much.
RAMON: Que?
CLAUDIUS: Gracias, gracias.
RAMON: Por nada. *—Eighth Joke, language barrier repeat*

Ramon goes back to work. Claudius does a take on how much money Ramon had, and then hands a dollar each to Rossencraft and Gilderstone. Rossencraft and Gilderstone make the correct replies, but Claudius is barely listening. He is remarking to the guards about the amount of money Ramon had on him.

—Ninth Joke, the King's simple nature

ROSSENCRAFT: Both your majesties might, by the sovereign power you have of us, put your dread pleasures more into command than to entreaty.
GILDERSTONE: But we both obey, and here give up ourselves in

the full bent to lay our service freely at your feet to be commanded.

CLAUDIUS [*already on his way out with the two guards, manages part of a thank you but still can't remember the second boy's name*]: Thanks Rossencraft and gentle—

GERTRUDE [*covers for him and then exits herself*]: Thanks, Gilderstone and gentle Rossencraft.

Rossencraft and Gilderstone are left alone with Ramon.

SCENE XIII: Hamlet Welcomes His Two Old Friends to Denmark

THE RAMON ROUTINE (PART III)

Rossencraft and Gilderstone decide to follow the King and Queen. As they start out, Ramon trips Gilderstone with his broom. —First Joke, slapstick

Rossencraft grabs Ramon from behind, and Gilderstone leaps to his feet ready to punch the insolent janitor in the nose.
—Joke set-up and insight into
Rossencraft and Gilderstone's
seedy nature

Gilderstone grabs Ramon by the hair as he makes ready to punch him, but the hair comes off; it is a wig.
—Second Joke, on Gilderstone

Ramon turns to Rossencraft who slowly removes the glasses and nose. He then turns to Gilderstone who reaches for the mustache, but Ramon tears it off and dances away in delight at his joke.
—Third Joke, grows slowly and moves
the audience's attention back into the
play as Rossencraft and Gilderstone
catch on and laugh.

Rehearsal note: The Rossencraft and Gilderstone scene which follows is a difficult one because in it Hamlet is already antic and joking with the words themselves. The scene was very helpful in rehearsals because it provided the first insight into Hamlet's character as a prankster, but if you let the scene rest on the words alone after the preceding frenetic activity, it will seem very dull and the movement of the play will drag. So your problem is to find pieces of business which are as alive as the words without obscuring what Hamlet is doing to his supposed friends in the scene.

THE OLD COLLEGE BANTER

which is carried out with a lot of handshaking and friendly pushing and shoving.

GILDERSTONE: My honored lord!

ROSSENCRAFT: My most dear lord!

HAMLET: My excellent good friends! How dost thou, Gilderstone? Ah, Rossencraft! Good lads, how do you both?

ROSSENCRAFT: As the indifferent children of the earth.

GILDERSTONE: Happy in that we are not over happy; on Fortune's cap we are not the very button.

HAMLET: Nor the soles of her shoe?

ROSSENCRAFT: Neither, my lord.

HAMLET: Then you live about her waist, or in the middle of her favors?

GILDERSTONE: Faith, her privates we.

HAMLET: In the secret parts of Fortune? O, most true; she is a strumpet. What news?

ROSSENCRAFT: None, my lord, but that the world's grown honest.

HAMLET POSES HIS QUESTION
FOR THE FIRST TIME

HAMLET: Then is doomsday near; but your news is not true. Let me question more in particular. What have you, my good friends, deserved at the hands of Fortune, that she sends you to prison hither?

GILDERSTONE: Prison, my lord!

HAMLET: Denmark's a prison.

ROSSENCRAFT: Then is the world one.

HAMLET [*speaks to the audience*]: A goodly one; in which there are many confines, wards, and dungeons, Denmark being one o' the worst.

ROSSENCRAFT: We think not so, my lord.

HAMLET: Why, then, 'tis none to you; for there is nothing either good or bad but thinking makes it so. To me it is a prison.

ROSSENCRAFT: Why, then your ambition makes it one; 'tis too narrow for your mind.

HAMLET [*laughing loudly, runs across the stage and tries to sit in his trash can. It tips over, spilling him to the floor. More laughter.*] O God, I could be bounded in a nutshell, and count myself a king of infinite space, were it not that I have bad dreams.

GILDERSTONE: Which dreams, indeed, are ambition, for the very substance of the ambitious is merely the shadow of a dream.

HAMLET: A dream itself is but a shadow. By my fay, I cannot reason. [*He begins to pick up the peanut bags which have spilled out of the trash can.*]

ROSSENCRAFT and GILDERSTONE [*stooping to help him*]: We'll wait upon you.

HAMLET [*slaps their hands, knocking the peanut bags, which they have picked up, back on the floor*]: No such matter. I will not sort you with the rest of my servants, for, to speak to you like an honest man, I am most dreadfully attended. [*He tosses a bag of peanuts to Claudius' bodyguard who has returned and is standing by the sliding doors watching over the scene.*]

HAMLET POSES HIS QUESTION FOR THE SECOND TIME

HAMLET: But in the beaten way of friendship, what make you at Elsinore?

ROSSENCRAFT: To visit you, my lord; no other occasion.

Hamlet picks up the broom and begins sweeping the upstage area behind the circular staircase.

HAMLET POSES HIS QUESTION YET A THIRD TIME

HAMLET: Beggar that I am, I am even poor in thanks, but I thank you: and sure, dear friends, my thanks are too dear a halfpenny. Were you not sent for? Is it your own inclining? Is it a free visitation? [*He slams the broom against the circular staircase, startling Rossencraft and Gilderstone with the loud clang. Threateningly*] Come, come, deal justly with me: come, come; nay speak.

GILDERSTONE: What should we say, my lord?

HAMLET: Why anything, but to the purpose. [*He coaxes them, pointing at them and laughing—change of pace.*] You were sent for and there is a kind of confession in your looks which your modesties have not craft enough to color. I know the good king and queen have sent for you.

ROSSENCRAFT: To what end, my lord?

HAMLET ASKS HIS QUESTION FOR THE LAST TIME AND GETS AN ANSWER

He holds out his hand thumb-up for the old fraternity handshake. With every phrase of his conjuring, one man grabs hold in turn until there is a stack of hands.

HAMLET: That you must teach me. But let me conjure you, by the rights of our fellowship, by the consonancy of our youth, by the obligation of our ever-preserved love, and by what more dear a better proposer could charge you withal [*he bends *their thumbs over painfully forcing them to the ground*] be even and direct with me whether you were sent for or no.

ROSSENCRAFT: What say you?

HAMLET [*more thumbscrews*]: Nay, if you love me, hold not off.

GILDERSTONE: My lord, we were sent for.

He lets them go and they collapse on the floor nursing their wounded thumbs. He then checks the up-center doors to make sure no one is listening. The guard begins to draw his gun and advance on Rossencraft and Gilderstone, but Hamlet hands him a bill and he slowly leaves.

HAMLET SEEMS TO EXPLAIN HIMSELF, BUT HIS FRIENDS DON'T UNDERSTAND

As his speech grows more rapturous, Hamlet begins to shed his Ramon clothes, throwing them over his shoulder so that they hit Rossencraft and Gilderstone.

HAMLET: I will tell you why; so shall my anticipation prevent your discovery, and your secrecy to the king and queen moult no feather. I have of late—but wherefore I know not—lost all my mirth, forgone all custom of exercises; and indeed it goes so heavily with my disposition that this goodly frame, the earth, seems to be a sterile promontory; this most excellent canopy, the air, look you, this brave o'erhanging firmament, this majestical roof fretted with golden fire, why, it appeareth nothing to me but a foul and pestilent congregation of vapors. [*He notices the audience and forgets about Rossencraft and Gilderstone entirely. He goes into the audience enthusiastically shaking hands with everyone he can reach.*] What a piece of work is a man! How noble in reason! how infinite in faculties! in form and moving how express and admirable! in action how like an angel! in apprehension how like a god! the beauty of the world, the paragon of animals. And yet to me what is this quintessence of dust? Man delights not me; no, nor woman neither [*he points to someone in the audience*], though by your smiling you seem to say so.

ROSSENCRAFT: My lord, there was no such stuff in my thoughts.

HAMLET [*turns on them angrily*]: Why did you laugh, then, when I said "man delights not me"? [*He again runs into the audience shaking hands and welcoming everyone to the theater.*] My good friends, you are welcome to Elsinore, to the castle, to New York City, to the New York Shakespeare Festival production of *Hamlet*! [*He returns to the stage at a dead run and grabs Rossencraft and Gilderstone each by the hand, spinning them in a circle.*] Your hands! come then; the appurtenance of welcome is but fashion and ceremony. [*He stops dead and looks them in the eye.*] You are welcome; but my uncle-father and aunt-mother are deceived.

ROSSENCRAFT: In what, my dear lord?

HAMLET: I am but mad north-north-west. When the wind is southerly, I know a hawk from a handsaw. [*He tosses his broom to Gilderstone and turns the trash basket upside down over Rossencraft's head.*]

ROSSENCRAFT: Good my lord!

HAMLET: I'll leave you till night. Goodbye to you!

All three run out the tunnel, Hamlet leading. Hamlet returns immediately.

SCENE XIV: Father and Son
Have an Idea

THE OLD ROPE BIT

When Hamlet returns to center stage, a rope is thrown from the tunnel and lands at his feet. He does a take and begins pulling on it. Out of the tunnel, at the other end of the rope, appears the Ghost, standing on Hamlet's coffin, which now has a lid, and wearing a magnificent gold helmet with horns. He smiles grandly and acknowledges the audience. When Hamlet gets to the end of the rope, he looks up and sees the Ghost.

HAMLET: Dad!
GHOST: My boy!

THE MUTUAL IDEA BIT

Both crouch down and rise slowly with each phrase.

GHOST: I have heard—
HAMLET: that guilty creatures—
GHOST: sitting at a play—
HAMLET: have by the very cunning of the scene—
GHOST: been struck so to the soul—
BOTH: that presently they have proclaimed their malefactions.
GHOST [*jumps off the coffin and speaks to the audience*]: For murder—
HAMLET [*also to audience*]: though it have no tongue—
GHOST: will speak—
BOTH: with most miraculous organ! [*They move to center where*

they join hands and bow.] The play's the thing, wherein we'll catch the conscience of the king! [*They point to Claudius, bow, and run off stage. The Ghost pauses for a moment to leave his gold, horned helmet on stage.*]

Claudius and Gertrude have entered above on the catwalk, and Rossencraft and Gilderstone are standing in the tunnel. They have all been watching the last few lines. Now Polonius enters on the catwalk, and Rossencraft and Gilderstone move onto the stage. Claudius questions them sternly.

SCENE XV: Claudius Is Concerned About Hamlet

Note: Do not spend a lot of time with this scene; it simply demonstrates Claudius' growing concern with Hamlet and establishes that Hamlet is going to put on a play. If you linger with this scene you will break the increasing tempo which is building toward the climax of the party scene.

A point of interest: Rossencraft has no way of knowing any more than Claudius what Hamlet is up to, but it is he who announces that Hamlet "means to give a play tonight." This inconsistency is an indication that Shakespeare's careful plotting of the melodramatic conspiracies and palace intrigue is no longer important in this production.

CLAUDIUS: And can you by no drift of conference get from him why he puts on this confusion, grating so harshly all his days of quiet with turbulent and dangerous lunacy?

ROSSENCRAFT: He does confess he feels himself distracted, but from what cause he will by no means speak.

GILDERSTONE: Nor do we find him forward to be sounded, but with a crafty madness keeps aloof, when we would bring him on to some confession of his true state.

GERTRUDE: Did he receive you well?

ROSSENCRAFT: Most like a gentleman.

GILDERSTONE: But with much forcing of his disposition.

ROSSENCRAFT: Niggard of question, but of our demands most free in his reply.

GERTRUDE: Did you assay him to any pastime?

ROSSENCRAFT: Madam, he means to give a play tonight.

POLONIUS: 'Tis most true; and he beseech'd me to entreat your majesties to hear and see the matter.

THE CLAUDIUS-IS-NOT-A-THEATERGOER BIT

CLAUDIUS: A *play?*

GERTRUDE: Oh Claudius, please can we go? [*She snuggles up to him.*]

CLAUDIUS: I don't want to go to any damned play.

GERTRUDE: Oh please, Claudius, say yes.

CLAUDIUS [*kisses his Queen on the neck and answers*]: With all my heart; and it doth much content me to hear him so inclined. Good gentlemen, give him a further edge, and drive his purpose into these delights.

ROSSENCRAFT: We shall, my lord.

Claudius and Gertrude exit above, followed by Polonius; Rossencraft and Gilderstone rush off below.

SCENE XVI: Getting Ready for the Party

SETTING THE STAGE

As Rossencraft and Gilderstone exit, the lights go to black and the theater is filled with loud rock music. A follow spot comes up and begins moving wildly about the stage in time with the music. Hamlet and the Ghost enter dancing and begin to set up the stage for the play within the play. The sliding doors open and two guards slide two low sawhorses on stage. Hamlet and the Ghost place these down right and then put the coffin lid and the coffin across them, forming a little stage of sorts. Two larger sawhorses are slid on and the father-son team sets them up left against one of the columns and places a wide plank across them. They then place two chairs on this improvised dais; one chair has a balloon that says QUEEN *on it, the other a balloon marked* KING. *Two guards enter from the down-left tunnel with a stair unit that they place in front of the dais. All of this activity is carried out with circus flourishes and dancing.*

A SHORT DANCE

Hamlet and his father begin dancing with some of the women and girls in the audience, leading them on stage. The guards join in.

SOME OLD ROUTINES

Hamlet and his father mount the dais still dancing while the follow spot begins to move rapidly up and down on them giving

*a stroboscopic effect. They begin to cross and uncross their legs
rapidly in time with the music and then to play a swift game of
patty-cake. At the same time the guards escort the ladies back to
their seats and exit.*

THE GHOST LEAVES: WAS HE EVER THERE?

*The Ghost moves slowly off the dais and off stage—while Hamlet
is left there still playing patty-cake. As the Ghost leaves, the
music begins to fade and the lights come up revealing Hamlet
playing patty-cake with the air. Horatio has entered from the
down-left tunnel pushing a tea caddy with party hats, favors, and
several cans of beer. Hamlet sees him and is a little embarrassed.*

HAMLET: Horatio!
HORATIO: At your service, my lord.

THE FINAL PREPARATIONS

*During this conversation, Hamlet begins to collect things he
needs for the party out of the coffin. He puts on a party hat, puts
a whistle around his neck, and loads his pockets with a cigar,
matches, and some party favors. Horatio has seated himself down
left with his guitar.*

HAMLET: Horatio, thou art e'en as just a man
  As e'er my conversation cop'd withal.
HORATIO: O' my dear lord—
HAMLET: Nay, do not think I flatter;
  For what advancement may I hope from thee,
  That no revenue hast but thy good spirits
  To feed and clothe thee? Why should the poor be flatter'd?
  No, let the candied tongue lick absurd pomp,
  And crook the pregnant hinges of the knee

Where thrift may follow fawning. Dost thou hear?
    Blest are those
Whose blood and judgement are so well comingled
That they are not a pipe for fortune's finger
To sound what stop she please. Give me that man
That is not passion's slave,

> [*He dangles a toy mouse by the tail.*]
    and I will wear him

In my heart's core, ay, in my heart of hearts
As I do thee.

> [*He puts the toy mouse in the breast pocket of his jacket. He hears Polonius and Ophelia off stage.*]
    Something to much of this.

SCENE XVII: Claudius Is Humiliated at Hamlet's Party

THE GUESTS GATHER

Polonius and Ophelia enter from the down-left tunnel, while Rossencraft and Gilderstone enter with a noisy group of guards from the other. Hamlet has Rossencraft and Gilderstone distribute beer and party favors to the guards who climb to the first level catwalk, laughing and talking. He then seats Ophelia on the improvised stage.

HAMLET: How now, my lord, will the king hear this piece of work?

POLONIUS: And the queen, too, and that presently.

HAMLET: Will you two help?

ROSSENCRAFT and GILDERSTONE: Ay, my lord.

HAMLET: Ophelia, will you sing for me tonight?

OPHELIA: Ay, my lord.

A JOKE ON POLONIUS

During this sequence Hamlet takes a movie camera from the tea caddy and begins filming the scene and the audience. The guards laugh at Polonius, throwing streamers at him as he postures about the stage.

HAMLET: My lord, you played once i' th' university, you say?

POLONIUS: That did I, my lord, and was accounted the best actor in the world, either for tragedy, comedy, history, pastoral,

pastoral-comical, historical-pastoral, tragical-historical, tragical-comical-historical-pastoral.

HAMLET: What did you enact?

POLONIUS: I did enact Julius Caesar. I was killed i' the Capitol. Brutus killed me.

HAMLET: It was a brute part of him to kill so capital a calf there.

A JOKE ON HAMLET

> *Note*: Early in rehearsal, this scene was filled with ominous overtones and sullen looks. There were thundering passages from the Ghost who delivered his threats over loudspeakers, and at one point a life-sized dummy of Hamlet's father went up in flames. Every line dripped with significance. Do not fall into this trap. A party is more appropriate, and Hamlet's jibes and ironies will stand by themselves. The party will take shape if everyone is in a good humor, and if you make sure that Hamlet initiates all the activities so that we see him constantly working on Claudius who is, of course, his object in the scene.

Claudius and Gertrude enter above and descend the circular staircase. Claudius is in his dress uniform. He is drunk. Gertrude is wearing a floor-length chiffon evening dress.

CLAUDIUS [*extending his hand warmly to Hamlet*]: How fares our cousin Hamlet?

Hamlet shakes the King's hand and BUZZZZZZ. The King had cleverly concealed a palm buzzer in his hand. Great laughter. Claudius proudly shows the buzzer to everyone.

A JOKE ON CLAUDIUS

HAMLET [*offers Claudius a cigar, which he takes*]: Excellent, i' faith; of the chameleon's dish. I eat the air, promise-crammed. You cannot feed capons so.

CLAUDIUS: I have nothing with this answer, Hamlet. These words are not mine.

HAMLET: No, nor mine now.

Hamlet lights the cigar for Claudius. BANG! It was an exploding cigar. Claudius laughs, everyone joins in, and the party is off to a fine start.

The Grand Processional

Hamlet blows his whistle to get everyone's attention, and he begins singing, Souza-band style, "Hail to the Chief" (the tune, no words). Everyone joins in; Hamlet leads Gertrude and Claudius in triumphal procession up to the dais. The guards throw more streamers; the King and Queen acknowledge the cheering throngs as they mount the stairs to their "thrones."

The Chug-a-Lug

Hamlet blows his whistle to stop the singing and pulls a bottle of Scotch off the tea caddy. He tosses it to the King and there is a great cheer. Claudius stands, tosses his hat to Gertrude, and pulls the stopper out of the bottle with his teeth. He takes a deep breath, holding the bottle at arm's length.

HAMLET: Do it, Denmark!

Claudius begins drinking, and Hamlet leads a long slow cheer which grows as Claudius keeps drinking. Gilderstone starts a drum roll on one of the metal columns. Claudius finishes with a flourish and tosses the bottle to his bodyguard. There is great cheering and applause.

HAMLET JOKES WITH OPHELIA
FOR CLAUDIUS' AMUSEMENT

Hamlet works between Claudius and Ophelia, delivering the lines to her and sharing the laughter with Claudius.

GERTRUDE: Come hither, my dear Hamlet, lie by me.
HAMLET: No, good mother, here's metal more attractive.
POLONIUS: O ho! do you mark that?
HAMLET: Lady, shall I lie in your lap?
OPHELIA: No, my lord.
HAMLET: I mean, my head upon your lap?
OPHELIA: Ay, my lord.
HAMLET: Do you think I meant country matters?
OPHELIA: I think nothing, my lord.

Hamlet shows Claudius a dirty picture and they share a laugh over it.

HAMLET: That's a fair thought to lie between maids' legs.

> *Note*: This technique of using a physical object to change the reference of a line is very useful.

OPHELIA: What is, my lord?
HAMLET: Nothing.
OPHELIA: You are merry, my lord.
HAMLET: Who, I?
OPHELIA: Ay, my lord.

THE JIG-MAKER

Hamlet introduces Claudius as "your only jig-maker" and begins to clap and stamp his feet in rhythm.

HAMLET: Oh God, Your only jig-maker!

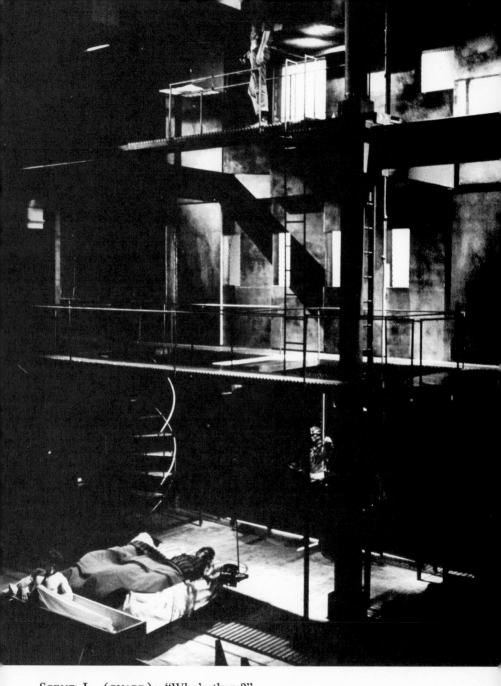

SCENE I (GUARD): "Who's there?"
Note Gertrude and Claudius in the Royal Bed, Hamlet in his coffin, and the guard at the top level of the catwalks. The sliding doors are directly behind the guard standing at stage level, and the circular staircase can be seen emerging from the shadows at left.

SCENE II   (CLAUDIUS): "Though yet of Hamlet our dear brother's death the memory be green . . ."

SCENE XII   (CLAUDIUS): "Welcome dear Rossencraft and gentle Gilderstone."

Scene XIII (HAMLET):
"What a piece of work
is a man!"

Scene XVII (HAMLET):
"O God your only jig-
maker!
This photograph is from the
Public's Theater's school
production. Cleavon Little
plays Hamlet; Edward
Setrakian, Claudius.

SCENE XVII (CLAUDIUS
and HAMLET singing): "Let
the galled jade wince . . ."

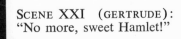

SCENE XXI (GERTRUDE):
"No more, sweet Hamlet!"

Scene XXVII (Ghost):
"What is a man,
If the chief good and
market of his time
Be but to sleep and feed?"

Scene XXIX (Hamlet):
"Rossencraft and
Gilderstone are dead!"

SCENE XXX (OPHELIA):
"By Gis and by
Saint Charity
Alack and fie for shame!"

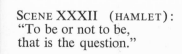

SCENE XXXII (HAMLET):
"To be or not to be,
that is the question."

SCENE XXXIII (HAMLET): "Not a whit, we defy augury."
This photograph is from the Public Theater's production, which toured the
neighborhoods of New York in the summer of 1968.

SCENE XXXIII (HAMLET): "A man's life is no more than to say
'One,' my lord."

SCENE XXXIII (HAMLET): "The readiness is all."
This photograph is from the school production.

Everyone joins in, shouting, stamping, and clapping in rhythm. Claudius takes off his coat, leaps off the dais, and begins a wild folk dance around the stage until he falls amid laughter and cheers. Hamlet films the event, but when Claudius falls, he turns the camera on his mother who comes forward smiling for the camera.

HAMLET: What should a man do but be merry? For look you how cheerfully my mother looks, and my father died within's two hours.

Everyone falls silent. Gertrude looks away, and we can hear the camera grinding.

HAMLET'S GOOD SPIRITS REVIVE AND THE PARTY CONTINUES

OPHELIA: Nay, 'tis twice two months, my lord.
HAMLET: So long? [*He rips off his black tie as a demonstration that he is no longer in mourning.*] Nay, then, let the devil wear black, for I'll have a suit of sables. O heavens! die two months ago and not forgotten yet? Then there's hope a great man's memory may outlive his life half a year.

THE MINCING MALICHO BIT

Hamlet puts the gold-horned helmet on Claudius who is now quite drunk and enjoying himself immensely.

CLAUDIUS: What means this, Hamlet?

Hamlet introduces Claudius to the guests as "Mincing Malicho," takes two balloons which are tied together with string from out of the coffin and puts them around Claudius' shoulders. Claudius begins to prance around, flaunting his pink and blue breasts as

Hamlet deftly lifts Claudius' gun from his shoulder holster. Claudius protests mildly but he is too drunk and having too much fun to really care.

HAMLET: Marry, this is Mincing Malicho. It means mischief.

OPHELIA [*nervously*]: Belike this show imports the argument of the play.

HAMLET [*indicates Claudius*]: We shall know by this fellow. We players cannot keep counsel; we'll tell all.

OPHELIA: Will you tell us what this show means?

HAMLET: Ay, or any show that you will show me. Be not you shamed to show, I'll not shame to tell you what it means.

OPHELIA: You are naught, you are naught.

HAMLET STARTS HIS SHOW

HAMLET [*mounts the stage as Horatio plays a flourish on his guitar*]:
> For us and for our tragedy,
> Here stooping to your clemency,
> We beg your hearing patiently.

How like you this prologue?

OPHELIA: 'Tis brief, my lord.

HAMLET [*tosses Claudius' coat, which has been lying on the stage, to the Queen*]: As woman's love.

THE FAIR OPHELIA INTRO

Hamlet brings Ophelia to the stage and asks her to sit down. He then has Claudius lie on the stage with his head and horns on Ophelia's lap, a role which Claudius enjoys.

HAMLET: I pray you.

OPHELIA: My lord?

HAMLET: I do beseech you. [*He tells everyone to be quiet, dims the lights, and whispers softly*] The fair Ophelia!

Ophelia sings her ballad, while Hamlet films her. Hamlet sings his response, and when Ophelia picks up the song again he moves into the audience, still filming. Everyone else slowly falls asleep.

OPHELIA: Woe is me. You are so sick of late.
So far from cheer and from your former state.

HAMLET: I must leave thee, love, and shortly too.
My operant powers their functions leave to do,
And thou shalt live in this fair world behind,
Honored, beloved and haply one as kind
For husband shalt thou—

OPHELIA: O confound the rest!
Such love must needs be treason in my breast.
In second husband let me be accurst;
None wed the second but who killed the first.

Hamlet is standing at the back of the house. He speaks softly. Ophelia then resumes her song.

HAMLET: Wormwood. Wormwood! I pray you, sing on.

OPHELIA [*sings*]: A second time I kill my husband dead,
When second husband kisses me in bed.
Both here and hence pursue me lasting strife,
If once awidow, ever I be wife.

Hamlet has returned to the stage. He quickly turns on the lights, claps and yells, "Bravo! Bravo!" Everyone wakes up and claps feebly. Claudius in the process falls off the stage, and Ophelia runs up center.

THE MOUSETRAP GAME

Gertrude is now a little drunk herself. Claudius is trying very hard to be serious, but Hamlet succeeds in keeping him in high spirits.

HAMLET: Madam, how like you this play?

GERTRUDE: The lady doth protest too much, methinks.

HAMLET: O, but she'll keep her word.

CLAUDIUS: Have you heard the argument? Is there no offence in it?

HAMLET: No, no, they do but jest—murder in jest. No offence in the world.

CLAUDIUS: What do you call the play?

HAMLET: The Mousetrap.

Hamlet pulls the toy mouse out of his pocket. Claudius grabs it, and with a huge laugh starts to chase Ophelia, who squeals and tries to escape by running around behind the circular staircase and then out the tunnel. Claudius trips and falls, to everyone's amusement and Ophelia's relief; Hamlet has to help him off the floor and seats him on the edge of the coffin.

HAMLET: The image of a murder done in Vienna. 'Tis a knavish piece of work. You shall see anon. But what of that? Your majesty and we that have free souls, it touches us not.

HAMLET and CLAUDIUS [*join in a drunken song*]:
Let the galled jade wince, our
withers are unwrung.

Hamlet tips Claudius back into the coffin.

A LAST JOKE ON OPHELIA

Hamlet picks up Ophelia and dumps her on top of Claudius. She squeals as Claudius tries to grab her.

OPHELIA: You are a good interpreter, my lord.

HAMLET: I could interpret between you and your love if I could see the poopies dallying.

OPHELIA: You are keen, my lord, you are keen.

HAMLET: It would cost you a groaning to take off mine edge.

OPHELIA: Still better, and worse.

HAMLET: So must you take your husbands. [*To Claudius, under Ophelia*] Ha, ha boy! Art thou there, true-penny?

GERTRUDE GETS INTO THE ACT

Madam, I pray *you*.

Gertrude comes forward and suddenly says her line to Claudius, who waves her away and keeps playing with Ophelia.

GERTRUDE: Sleep rock thy brain, and never come mischance between us twain.

CLAUDIUS' BIG CHANCE TO BE A STAR

Hamlet gives his camera to Horatio, and hands Ophelia a copy of the Hamlet *text from which Claudius will read. He indicates that it is now Claudius' turn to act and signals everyone to be quiet. Claudius sits up and tries to focus on the text. Then in a great voice he begins.*

CLAUDIUS: To be or not to be, that is—

HAMLET [*interrupts, laughing*]: Nay, nay, my lord, here. [*He indicates a different place in the text.*]

CLAUDIUS: O.K., Hamlet. Take two?

HAMLET: Ay, my lord. Come on, murderer, begin.

Hamlet motions for Horatio to begin filming, and Claudius stands in the coffin. Ophelia takes this opportunity to get away, and she runs up stage. Claudius reads in the old Shakespearean manner, slowing down only for the last line which he reads very deliberately as he begins to understand what he has said.

CLAUDIUS: O what a falling-off was there! From me, whose love was of that dignity that it went hand in hand even with the vow I made to her in marriage—and to decline upon a wretch whose natural gifts were poor to those of mine!—to sate herself in a celestial bed and prey on garbage. Thus was I, by a brother's hand, of life, of crown, of queen, at once dispatch'd.

During Claudius' speech Hamlet has mounted the dais, and Gertrude has helped him put on Claudius' dress coat and hat. He is now sitting next to his mother who is holding his arm. He strikes a match and pops the King balloon. Claudius throws down the text and turns to look at Hamlet. Hamlet laughs and begins speaking. He will move off the dais and talk sometimes to the audience, sometimes to particular characters.

HAMLET'S TRIUMPH

HAMLET [*laughing*]: O, what a rogue and peasant slave am I! Is it not monstrous that this *player* here, but in a *fiction*, in a *dream* of passion, can force his soul so to his own conceit that from her working all his visage wanned, tears in his eyes, distraction in his aspect, a broken voice, and his whole function suiting with forms to his conceit? And all for nothing . . . for nothing! [*He throws Claudius' dress hat at him with a laugh.*] What would he do had he the motive and the cue for passion that I have? He would drown the stage with tears, and cleave the general ear with horrid speech, make mad the guilty and appal the free, confound the ignorant, and amaze indeed the very faculties of eyes and ears. [*He sits next to his mother and tearfully buries his head in her lap.*] Yet I, a dull and muddy-mettled rascal, peak, like John-a-dreams, unpregnant of my cause, and can say nothing. [*He stamps his foot and shouts.*] No, not for a king, upon whose property and most dear life a damned defeat was made. Am I a coward? [*He pulls out the gun he stole from Claudius and slowly moves down to confront the King. Instantly the guards react, some pulling their own guns, but Claudius signals them not to do anything yet.*] Who calls me villain? Breaks my pate across? Plucks off my beard and blows it in my face? Tweaks me by the nose? Gives me the lie i' the throat as deep as to the lungs? Who does me this? Ha, 'swounds, I should take it, for it cannot be but I am pigeon-livered, and lack gall to make oppression bitter, or ere this I should have fatted all the region kites with this slave's offal. [*He points the gun at Claudius.*] Bloody, bawdy villain! Remorseless, treacherous, lecherous, kindless villain!

Hamlet Breaks Up the Play

> *Note:* You will of course have to improvise the next section yourself in rehearsal, but we include here a description of the scene as it generally occurred in our production.

Hamlet shoots Claudius. Everyone is startled. Ralph Waite (Claudius) is furious and yells, "What the hell was that?" to Marty (Hamlet) who is laughing and talking to Michael Heit (Horatio). Everyone begins talking angrily, and suddenly Ralph lunges for Marty, tearing apart the improvised stage in the process and throwing the coffin to the floor. Marty strips off his military jacket, ready to go for Ralph, but both are restrained by some of the other actors. The stage is in chaos. "You little bastard, what's the idea?" "That's the third time you've pulled that." "Let me at the little son of a bitch."

Gradually order is restored, and Ralph agrees to take the last moment again. As Marty starts his last line, Ralph erupts and yells, "No, I'm not going to do it. I don't have to take that kind of crap." He stalks off stage pursued by most of the other actors trying to get him back. The few that are left on stage don't know what to do and exit in confusion. Only Marty and Michael Heit are left. Marty blows his whistle, laughs and cries,

VENGEANCE!

He exits laughing while Michael remains on stage filming the audience. Over the loudspeakers we hear Marty's voice laughing and saying, "Vengeance, vengeance, vengeance, vengeance, vengeance," and backstage Ralph Waite is heard still arguing vehemently. As Marty's laughter dies away, he re-enters, smoking a cigar and singing. He sings to the audience or to Horatio. Backstage, the argument continues through the song.

HAMLET [*sings*]: Why, let the stricken deer go weep,
  The heart ungalled play;
  For some must watch, while some must sleep;
  Thus runs the world away.
  For thou dost know, O Damon dear,
  This realm dismantled was
  Of Jove himself; and now reigns here
  A very, very—pajock.

The sliding doors are thrown open and Ralph runs on stage dragging two or three guards with him and yelling at Marty. Marty runs into the tunnel until Ralph is restrained by the guards and Rossencraft and Gilderstone and is pulled back off stage. The doors are closed, and Rossencraft and Gilderstone remain. Hamlet picks up his song again at Horatio's request.

HORATIO: You might have rhymed.
HAMLET [*sings*]:
  For if the King like not the comedy,
  Why then, belike he likes it not, perdy.

> *Note*: Audiences will believe that the fight is real for varying lengths of time, but it is essential that they be confused at least for a while. The point you are trying to make is about Hamlet's triumph and Claudius' humiliation; Marty's prank and Ralph's loss of composure. You will find that this climactic moment of the play will not sustain itself if it is done within

the context of the action of the play alone. Because you have been treating every moment in the play in a very special way, you must also treat this moment, and the most effective way to do this is to break the form of the play itself. You have already prepared the audience for the shattering of the play by the peanut scene and other colloquial moments. You will be able to make good use of the shattered focus of the play in the final section where all plot seems to disappear.

SCENE XVIII: Hamlet Savors His Triumph

Style note: As in the first Rossencraft and Gilderstone scene, the words themselves express Hamlet's antic character, but here you may let them work by themselves because a more relaxed scene is required after the preceding catastrophe. In fact the scene was largely improvised. Just make sure Rossencraft and Gilderstone give Hamlet enough room. They are a little afraid of him by now in any case. Horatio sits by and listens while Hamlet plays with his prey, occasionally cleaning up part of the mess from the party.

GILDERSTONE: Good my lord, vouchsafe me a word with you.

HAMLET: Sir, a whole history.

GILDERSTONE: The King, sir—

HAMLET: Ay, sir, what of him?

GILDERSTONE: Is in his retirement marvellous distempered.

HAMLET: With drink, sir?

GILDERSTONE: No, my lord, with choler.

HAMLET: Your wisdom should show itself more richer to signify this to the doctor; for, for me to put him to his purgation would perhaps plunge him into more choler.

GILDERSTONE: Good my lord, put your discourse into some frame, and start not so wildly from my affair.

HAMLET: I am tame, sir; pronounce.

GILDERSTONE: The queen, your mother, in most great affliction of spirit, hath sent me to you.

HAMLET: You are welcome.

GILDERSTONE: Nay, good my lord, this courtesy is not of the right breed. If it shall please you to make me a wholesome answer,

I will do your mother's commandment; if not, your pardon
and my return shall be the end of my business.

HAMLET: Sir, I cannot.

*Gilderstone gives up and moves away. Rossencraft adopts a more
self-righteous tone with Hamlet, and Hamlet becomes more
stern with him after a while.*

ROSSENCRAFT: What, my lord?

HAMLET: Make you a wholesome answer. My wit's diseased; but,
sir, such answer as I can make, you shall command; or, rather,
as you say, my mother. Therefore no more, but to the matter.
My mother, you say—

ROSSENCRAFT: Then, thus she says: your behaviour hath struck
her into amazement and admiration.

HAMLET: O wonderful son, that can so 'stonish a mother! But is
there no sequel at the heels of this mother's admiration?
Impart.

ROSSENCRAFT: She desires to speak with you ere you go to bed.

HAMLET: We shall obey, were she ten times our mother. Have
you any further trade with us?

ROSSENCRAFT: My lord, you once did love me.

HAMLET: And do still, by these pickers and stealers.

ROSSENCRAFT: Good my lord, what is your cause of distemper?
You do surely bar the door upon your own liberty, if you
deny your griefs to your friend.

HAMLET: Sir, I lack advancement.

ROSSENCRAFT: How can that be when you have the voice of the
king himself for your succession in Denmark?

HAMLET: Ay, sir, but "While the grass grows." [*He asks the
audience if anyone knows the end of the proverb. No one does,
so he continues. He has decided to make an end to the scene.*]
The proverb is something musty.

THE PIPE BIT

Hamlet picks up a plastic recorder, and taking his leave of Rossencraft, goes to Gilderstone who is leaning against the circular staircase. He speaks pleasantly to him and laughs off his answers.

HAMLET: Why do you go about to recover the wind of me as if you would drive me into a toil?

GILDERSTONE: O! my lord, if my duty be too bold, my love is too unmannerly.

HAMLET: I do not well understand that. Will you play upon this pipe?

GILDERSTONE: My lord, I cannot.

HAMLET: I pray you.

GILDERSTONE: Believe me, I cannot.

HAMLET: I do beseech you.

GILDERSTONE: I know no touch of it, my lord.

HAMLET: It is as easy as lying. Govern these ventages with your fingers and thumb, give it breath with your mouth, and it will discourse most eloquent music. Look you, these are the stops. [*He gives the pipe to Gilderstone.*]

GILDERSTONE: But these cannot I command to any utterance of harmony. I have not the skill.

Gilderstone nervously offers the pipe to Hamlet, who snatches it away, and with a jerk of the head, tells Gilderstone to move up stage. Hamlet then speaks evenly to the audience.

HAMLET: Why, look you now, how unworthy a thing you make of me. You would play upon me; you would seem to know my stops; you would pluck out the heart of my mystery; you would sound me from my lowest note to the top of my compass. And there is much music, excellent voice, in this little organ, yet cannot you make it speak. 'Sblood, do you think I am easier to be played on than a pipe? Call me what instrument you will, though you can fret me, yet you cannot play upon me.

THE CLOUD BIT

Hamlet by this time is very angry, but he changes his tone immediately on Polonius' entrance.

POLONIUS: My Lord!

HAMLET [*jovially*]: God bless you, sir!

POLONIUS: My lord, the queen would speak with you, and presently.

HAMLET [*points to Rossencraft*]: Do you see yonder cloud that's almost in shape of a camel?

POLONIUS: By the mass, and 'tis like a camel, indeed.

HAMLET [*points to Gilderstone*]: Methinks it is like a weasel.

POLONIUS: It is backed like a weasel.

HAMLET [*points again to Rossencraft*]: Or like a whale?

POLONIUS: Very like a whale.

HAMLET [*laughs and goes to talk with Horatio*]: Then I will come to my mother by and by. Horatio, they fool me to the top of my bent. I will come by and by.

POLONIUS: I will say so.

HAMLET: By and by is easily said. Leave me, friends.

Rossencraft, Gilderstone, and Polonius exit silently. Hamlet turns again to Horatio, who takes a gun out of his back pocket, twirls it, and hands it to Hamlet.

HAMLET: Good night, Horatio.

HORATIO: Good night unto your lordship. [*He exits pushing the tea caddy.*]

> *A possible gag*: On occasion Hamlet played that he couldn't remember Horatio's name, which is an interesting comment on the usual interpretation of Hamlet and Horatio as close friends.

SCENE XIX: Hamlet Is Still Alone (II)

A word of advice: You mustn't let the audience relax too long. They were partially alerted by Hamlet's unkind speech in the previous scene, but now you must prepare them for the rest of the play.

The lights dim as Horatio exits and Hamlet climbs the circular staircase.

HAMLET: 'Tis now the very witching time of night,
When churchyards yawn and hell itself breathes out
Contagion to this world. Now could I drink hot blood,
And do such bitter business as the day
Would quake to look on.

THE WAKE 'EM UP GAG

Hamlet fires his gun into the air. Your audience will be considerably startled by this.

THE OLD STUFFED DUCK GAG
WITH A NEW TWIST

A huge Panda bear falls out of the air onto the stage. Your audience will also be considerably startled by this and will laugh. They are waking up. Hamlet looks up in the air to see if anything else will fall, then shrugs his shoulders.

A REPEAT ON THE RAMON GAG

HAMLET [*in his Spanish Ramon accent*]: Soft now, to my mudder.

AN INTERLUDE

Immediately there is a burst of circus music, and the stage goes black except for the follow spot on the Panda. The follow spot begins its dance routine and the guards clean up the play within the play, taking off all sawhorses and planks.

> *Audience note*: You will find that the three quick gags at the end of the last scene, and this burst of activity, will have rejuvenated your audience. As in an earlier section of the play, when you wanted to re-establish the coherence of the plot, you have Claudius make a big entrance through the sliding doors.

SCENE XX: Osric Reports from Norway While Rossencraft and Gilderstone Find Out What Life Is Really Like

As the music fades, the lights come up and Claudius throws open the sliding doors. He strides on examining a tangled maze of exposed film. At the same time two guards bring in Rossencraft and Gilderstone unceremoniously. A third guard hustles on Horatio, and Osric appears at the down-right tunnel. He is wearing a fur hat and a great coat, and is quite enthusiastic about what he has to report. Claudius' attention is, however, fixed on the film and Horatio.

CLAUDIUS: Say, Osric, what news from Norway?

OSRIC: Your majesty, he has suppressed his nephew's levies which he says appeared to him a preparation against the Polack. But, better looked into, he truly found it was against your highness.

CLAUDIUS: The old fox. Proceed you.

OSRIC: He sent out arrests on Fortinbras, which he in brief obeys and makes vow before his uncle never more to give the assay of arms against your majesty.

CLAUDIUS: This likes us well. What more?

OSRIC: Old Norway has given Fortinbras three score thousand—

THE REPEATED INTERRUPTION BIT (PART I)

Claudius suddenly throws the film in Horatio's face. Horatio grabs the camera which a guard has been holding and begins once again to film Claudius. Claudius yells, "Get him outta here!" and shoves him out the tunnel. He is further escorted by a guard. Claudius grabs Rossencraft by the collar and hurls him across the stage.

CLAUDIUS: I like him not! [*He then throws Gilderstone to the ground.*] Nor stands it safe with us to let his madness range. Say, Osric!

OSRIC: Old Norway has given Fortinbras three score—

THE REPEATED INTERRUPTION BIT (PART II)

CLAUDIUS [*deliberately moves closer to Rossencraft and Gilderstone and speaks very slowly to them*]: Therefore prepare you. I your commission herewith dispatch, and Hamlet to England shall along with you. Say, Osric!

OSRIC: Old Norway has given Fort—

THE REPEATED INTERRUPTION BIT (PART III)

Claudius takes two guns from the guards who are standing near and shoves them in front of Rossencraft and Gilderstone. They slowly take them.

CLAUDIUS: Arm you, I pray you to this speedy voyage; for we will fetters put about this fear, which now goes too free-footed. Say, Osric!

OSRIC [*intimidated*]: Old Norway has given Fortinbras three score thousand crowns in annual fee and his commission to employ those soldiers so levied as before, against the Polack, and requests your pleasure to give them quiet pass through your dominions for this enterprise.

CLAUDIUS: Our armies will meet the restless Fortinbras at the border with allowance for his safe passage through Denmark. Go tell him so. [*He signals two guards to escort Osric out.*

Then he turns to Rossencraft and Gilderstone and grabs Rossencraft by the chin, forcing him to look at him.] I like him not!

Claudius exits quickly out the tunnel followed by his bodyguard. Two guards linger until Rossencraft and Gilderstone slowly stand and slowly exit without looking at each other.

SCENE XXI: Hamlet Kills Polonius and Drives His Mother Crazy

The lights brighten, revealing Hamlet at the third level of cat-walks. The sliding doors open and two guards bring on a table set up for a child's birthday party with a green paper tablecloth and various party favors. Gertrude enters in her chiffon night-gown from the first scene, laden with party hats, crepe-paper streamers, a music box, and a KING balloon. The music box is playing and she is in a gay, frivolous mood.

THE SET-UP

Polonius enters, all business, but Gertrude scarcely pays any attention to him as she begins setting up the party for her son. She does give him the KING balloon.

POLONIUS: He will come straight. Look you lay home to him. Tell him his pranks have been too broad to bear with, and that your Grace hath screened and stood between much heat and him.

HAMLET: Mother!

POLONIUS: I'll silence me under here. Pray you, be round with him.

GERTRUDE: I warrant you; fear me not.

HAMLET: Mother! Mother! Mother!

GERTRUDE: I hear him coming.

Polonius has hidden himself under the table, taking the balloon with him.

THE PEACEFUL SEQUENCE

Gertrude sees Hamlet above. He wears a party hat and is eating peanuts. They wave to each other and speak sweetly; Gertrude tries to lure Hamlet down to her party, showing him the tinkling music box and stringing crepe paper between the table and the railings at the aisle of the theater. Sometimes she speaks to the audience, confiding in them as fellow parents. Sometimes she gently chides Hamlet.

HAMLET: How is't with you, mother?

GERTRUDE: How is't with you?

HAMLET: Now, mother, what's the matter?

GERTRUDE: Hamlet, thou hast thy father much offended.

HAMLET: Mother, you have my father much offended.

GERTRUDE: Come, come, you answer with an idle tongue.

HAMLET: Go, go, you question with a wicked tongue.

GERTRUDE: Why, how now, Hamlet?

HAMLET: What's the matter now?

GERTRUDE: Have you forgot me?

HAMLET: No, by the rood, not so. You are the queen, your husband's brother's wife. And would it were not so—you are my mother.

A MORE HAZARDOUS SEQUENCE

Hamlet throws a handful of peanuts at his mother. She feigns anger and with little running steps pretends that she is leaving.

GERTRUDE: Nay then, I'll set those to you that can speak. [*Hamlet draws his gun. Gertrude looks around and sees it.*] What wilt thou do? Thou wilt not murder me? Help, ho! [*She runs out the down-left tunnel crying for help.*]

POLONIUS [*emerges from under the table still carrying the balloon*]: What, ho! Help, help, help!

HAMLET [*shoots Polonius as he runs for the exit*]: How now! A rat? Dead for a ducat dead!

Polonius cries out in pain and releases the balloon. He waves good-bye to the balloon as it floats up to the ceiling and slowly exits with a smile on his face.

POLONIUS: God be wi' ye, God be wi' ye.

The Confusion of Identities Bit

Gertrude runs across the stage and looks up at the balloon; Hamlet also tries to see the balloon from his catwalk.

GERTRUDE: O me, what hast thou done?

HAMLET: Nay, I know not, is it the king?

GERTRUDE: O, what a rash and bloody deed is this!

HAMLET: A bloody deed. Almost as bad, good mother, as kill a king and marry with his brother.

GERTRUDE: As kill a king?

The First Barrage of Peanuts

Hamlet accompanies the following tirade with handfuls of peanuts, while Gertrude tries to maintain her composure by protesting her innocence to the audience and attempting to ignore the fact that the peanuts keep hitting her.

HAMLET: Ay, lady, it was my word. Leave wringing of your hands and let me wring your heart.

GERTRUDE: What have I done, that thou dar'st wag thy tongue in noise so rude against me?

HAMLET: Such an act that blurs the grace and blush of modesty, calls virtue hypocrite, takes off the rose from the fair forehead of an innocent love and sets a blister there—makes marriage vows as false as dicers' oaths.

GERTRUDE: Ay me, what act, that roars so loud and thunder in the index?

HAMLET'S LECTURE

During this speech Hamlet operates two shadow boxes which are high in the darkness at the back of the stage. Each contains a large transparency, one of Hamlet's father, the other of Claudius, both in military uniform. He turns on one, then the other, as he talks about them, sometimes flashing them on and off for emphasis. At the end of the lecture he leaves them both on, and they remain on throughout the rest of the play. Below, Gertrude scans the audience, looking in the crowd for whomever it is Hamlet is talking about.

HAMLET: Look here, upon this picture, and on this: This was your husband. Look you now what follows. Here is your husband, like a mildew'd ear, a look fit for a murder and a rape, a dull, dead hanging look, and a hell-bred eye, to affright children and amaze the world. Have you eyes? Could you on this fair mountain leave to feed, and batten on this moor? Ha, have you eyes? You cannot call it love, for at your age the hey-day in the blood is tame, it's humble, and waits upon the judgement. And what judgement would step from this to this?

GERTRUDE: O Hamlet, speak no more! Thou turn'st my very eyes into my soul.

THE SECOND BARRAGE OF PEANUTS

The lecture has obviously had no effect on his mother so Hamlet again begins to pelt her with peanuts, harder and harder as the sequence continues. Gertrude begins to gather up the peanuts he has thrown and to toss them back at him, sometimes playfully, sometimes in earnest.

HAMLET: Nay, but to live in the rank sweat of an ensemened bed, stew'd in corruption, honeying and making love over the nasty sty—
GERTRUDE: O, speak to me no more! No more, sweet Hamlet!
HAMLET: A murderer and a villain, a slave that is not twentieth part the tithe of your precedent lord, a vice of kings, a cutpurse of the empire and the rule, that from a shelf the precious diadem stole and put it in his pocket!
GERTRUDE: No more!

Gertrude makes a last determined effort to hit Hamlet with the peanuts, throwing them underhand with a mighty effort, but they all go into the audience. She hides under the table.

THE GHOST SETS HAMLET BACK TO HIS TASK

The Ghost has entered previously, striding across the catwalk, apparently on some matter of importance. He is dressed in military hat, jacket and underwear, and he has watched part of the preceding peanut fight. As Hamlet is about to throw the whole bag of peanuts at Gertrude, the Ghost interrupts.

HAMLET: A king of shreds and patches . . .
GHOST: Uh-uh-uh, Hamlet!
HAMLET: What would your gracious figure?
GERTRUDE [*peeks out from under the table and then kneels beside it, hastily shelling and eating peanuts*]: Alas, he is mad!

Hamlet lets down the swing his father used on his last official visit. The Ghost pushes it away.

HAMLET: O say!
GHOST: No more of that! Do not forget. This visitation is but to whet thy almost blunted purpose. But look, amazement on thy mother sits. Speak to her Hamlet.

THE WHO'S-CRAZY SEQUENCE

As Hamlet speaks to her, Gertrude picks up the Panda, which is still lying on stage where it fell when Hamlet shot it, and speaks to it as if it were Hamlet. She then picks up her music box and holds it to her ear, swaying to the music.

HAMLET: How is it with you, lady?

GERTRUDE: Alas, how is't with you? Whereon do you look?

HAMLET: On him, on him! Do you see nothing there?

GERTRUDE: Nothing at all; yet all that is I see.

HAMLET: Nor did you nothing hear?

GERTRUDE: No, nothing but ourselves.

HAMLET: Why, look you there! look. My father in his habit as he liv'd! [*He throws the bag of peanuts at his father who catches them. He then climbs down a ladder to where the Ghost is standing.*]

GERTRUDE: This is the very coinage of your brain: this bodiless creation ecstasy is very cunning in.

HAMLET: Ecstasy! Mother, for love of grace, lay not that flattering unction to your soul, that not your trespass but my madness speaks.

GERTRUDE: O Hamlet, thus hast cleft my heart in twain.

GHOST: Hear me.

HAMLET: Hear me! Go not to my uncle's bed; assume a virtue, if you have it not. Refrain to-night, and that shall lend a kind of easiness to the next abstinence:

GHOST: the next more easy.

HAMLET [*directly to his father*]: I must to England; you know that?

GERTRUDE: Alack! I had forgot. 'Tis so concluded on.

HAMLET: And my two schoolfellows, whom I will trust as I will adders fang'd, they bear the mandate; they must sweep my way and marshal me to knavery. Let it work, for 'tis the sport to have the enginer hoist with his own petar; and 't shall go hard. [*He shakes hands good-bye with the Ghost and climbs down the circular staircase to stage level.*] But I will delve one yard below their mines and blow them at the moon. [*He fires off his gun. Gertrude starts, but goes on listening to her music box. Hamlet then picks up the Panda and throws it over his shoulder. He gives his mother a good-bye kiss on the forehead and starts out the tunnel.*] This man shall set me packing. I'll lug the guts into the neighbor room. Mother, good night.

The Ghost calls after Hamlet as he exits, but Hamlet tells him to be quiet because his mother is resting.

GHOST: Remember me!
HAMLET: Shhh!
GHOST [*whispers his plea and exits in frustration*]: Remember me!

There is a brief pause in which we hear only the music box.

SCENE XXII: Claudius in Pursuit of Hamlet

The sliding doors are thrown open and Claudius enters, followed by Rossencraft, Gilderstone, and the guards.

CLAUDIUS: Gertrude! Gertrude! Where is your son?
GERTRUDE: Bestow this place on us awhile.

Claudius signals for the others to leave. The bodyguard closes the door and remains on stage.

THE ALWAYS-HUMOR-A-MADWOMAN BIT

Gertrude begins dancing to the tune from her music box. Claudius begins dancing with her. She has a secret which she coyly refuses to tell him.

GERTRUDE: Ah, mine own lord, what have I seen tonight!
CLAUDIUS: Gertrude? How does Hamlet?
GERTRUDE: Mad as the sea. In his lawless fit, cries "a rat, a rat!" and kills the good old man.
CLAUDIUS: It had been so with us, had we been there. His liberty is full of threats to all—to you yourself, to us, to everyone. Where is he gone?
GERTRUDE: To draw apart the body he hath kill'd.

Claudius signals to his bodyguard to let the others in. When they are inside, Claudius, still dancing with Gertrude, speaks with them.

CLAUDIUS: My lords! Go join you with some further aid. Hamlet in madness hath Polonius slain. Go seek him out, speak fair, and bring the body into the chapel. I pray you, haste in this.

All the guards, Rossencraft, and Gilderstone run off in various directions. Claudius dances Gertrude out the tunnel as the lights fade to black.

SCENE XXIII: The Chase

In the darkness we hear guards calling out for Hamlet. Some of them appear on stage and in the audience with flashlights.

THE CORDLESS ELECTRIC RAZOR BIT

There is the sound of an electric razor going in the audience. It is Hamlet who has taken a seat and is shaving.

HAMLET: Who calls on Hamlet?

All the flashlights focus on Hamlet, as the guards and Rossencraft begin slowly to close in on him. When they reach him, he gets up and begins to move to the stage, the guards following. Hamlet turns off the razor when he is speaking, and he turns it back on again whenever Rossencraft speaks.

ROSSENCRAFT: What have you done, my lord, with the dead body?

HAMLET: Compounded it with dust, whereto 'tis kin.

ROSSENCRAFT: Tell us where 'tis, that we may take it thence and bear it to the chapel.

HAMLET: Do not believe it.

ROSSENCRAFT: Believe what?

HAMLET: That I can keep your counsel and not mine own. Besides, to be demanded of a sponge, what replication should be made by the son of a king.

ROSSENCRAFT: Take you me for a sponge, my lord?

HAMLET: Ay, sir, that soaks up the king's countenance, his rewards, his authorities. But such officers do the king best service in the end. He keeps them, like an ape an apple, in the corner of his jaw; first mouthed, to be last swallowed. When he needs what you have gleaned, it is but squeezing you, and, sponge, you shall be dry again.

ROSSENCRAFT: I understand you not, my lord.

HAMLET: I am glad of it. A knavish speech sleeps in a foolish ear.

ROSSENCRAFT: My lord, you must tell us where the body is, and go with us to the king.

HAMLET: The body is with the king, but the king is not with the body. The king is a thing—

THE TELEPHONE BIT

(a) The set-up. Hamlet reaches the stage and Gilderstone helps him down the last step which is unlighted.

GILDERSTONE: A thing, my lord!

HAMLET: Of nothing. Bring me to him.

(b) A telephone bell rings.

Oops, that's for me.

(c) Hamlet moves to the party table and picks up two small party horns, holding one to his ear and one to his mouth. He laughs and chuckles.

Hello? Oh yes, marvellous, marvellous.

(d) He holds out the horns to Gilderstone who takes them but doesn't seem to hear anything.

It's for you.

(e) Gilderstone is still listening at the telephone, and all the others are watching him. Hamlet runs for the nearest exit.

Hide fox, and all after!

(f) Gilderstone throws down the horns, and they all start after Hamlet.

SCENE XXIV: The Interrogation

The lights come up full, and we see that Hamlet has run into Claudius. He is captured.

CLAUDIUS: Now Hamlet, where's Polonius?

THE ALWAYS-HUMOR-A-MADMAN BIT (PART II) BUT NEVER HUMOR HAMLET

Hamlet seats Claudius at the party table, puts a party hat on him, and tucks a napkin into his collar. He then lights a candle which is on the table.

HAMLET: At supper.

CLAUDIUS: At supper! Where?

HAMLET: Not where he eats, but where 'a is eaten. A certain convocation of politic worms are e'en at him. Your worm is your only emperor for diet: we fat all creatures else to fat us, and we fat ourselves for maggots. Your fat king and your lean beggar is but variable service—two dishes, but to one table. That's the end. [*Hamlet holds out the match with which he lit the candle. Claudius blows it out.*]

CLAUDIUS: Alas, alas!

HAMLET [*begins filling a paper cup with peanuts for Claudius*]: A man may fish with the worm that hath eat of a king, and eat of the fish that hath fed of that worm.

CLAUDIUS: What dost thou mean by this?

HAMLET: Nothing, but to show you how a king may go a progress through the guts of a beggar.

Hamlet holds the cup out to Claudius, who knocks it away and lunges for Hamlet. Hamlet dodges around to the other side of the table, and they slowly circle, keeping the table between them.

CLAUDIUS: Where is Polonius?

HAMLET: In heaven. Send thither to see. If your messenger find him not there, seek him i' th' other place yourself. But, indeed, if you find him not within this month, you shall nose him as you go up the stairs into the lobby.

THE WHO-ME BIT

CLAUDIUS: Go seek him there.

Hamlet starts to leave.

No not you. *You!* Go! [*He points to two guards and they run out.*]

HAMLET: He will stay 'till you come.

THE NOW-YOU-SEE-HIM-NOW-YOU-DON'T BIT

As Claudius speaks, Hamlet begins to moan and falls to his knees in prayer so that his head disappears below the table. Claudius looks under the table, Hamlet looks up, Claudius looks up, Hamlet ducks under. Finally Claudius slams his fists on the table, Hamlet jumps up, and Claudius is able to finish his speech.

CLAUDIUS: Hamlet, this deed, for thine especial safety—which we do tender, as we dearly grieve for that which thou hast done—must send thee hence with fiery quickness. Therefore prepare thyself. Thy associates tend, and everything is bent for England.

HAMLET: For England?

CLAUDIUS: Ay, Hamlet.

HAMLET: Good.

CLAUDIUS: So is it, if thou knew'st our purposes.

Hamlet Makes a Confusing Exit

He pinches Rossencraft on the cheek, and then jumps up between Rossencraft and Gilderstone. They catch him and hold him in a fireman's carry.

HAMLET: I see a cherub that sees them. But, come; for England! Farewell, dear mother.

CLAUDIUS: Thy loving father, Hamlet.

Hamlet jumps down and shakes hands with a husband and wife in the audience. He then runs out the aisle, shaking hands and waving good-bye to all.

HAMLET: My mother. Father and mother is man and wife, man and wife is one flesh, and so, my mother. Farewell! For England!

CLAUDIUS: [*pushes Rossencraft and Gilderstone out after Hamlet*]: Follow him at foot. Tempt him with speed abroad. I'll have him hence tonight.

SCENE XXV: Claudius Shows
His True Nature

The NORWEGIAN CAPTAIN *enters on the first level of catwalks above, as the guards strike the party table. Claudius' bodyguard remains, standing beside Claudius holding the candle which he has taken from the table.*

CAPTAIN: My lord, thanks from the King of Norway for the promised safe passage of his forces. We are at rest hard by.

CLAUDIUS: I will grant but four days for your journey. The times are on edge.

CAPTAIN: My men are weary, my lord.

CLAUDIUS: Bid them make haste.

CAPTAIN: Ay, my lord.

CLAUDIUS: Fare you well.

THE MAN-OF-IRON BIT

Claudius snuffs out the candle with his bare hand. It hurts and he exits blowing on the sore and shaking his hand. The bodyguard follows.

CLAUDIUS: The present death of Hamlet. For like the hectic in my blood he rages. Till I know 'tis done, howe'er my haps, my joys were ne'er begun.

SCENE XXVI: Hamlet and His Father Have a Conversation with the Norwegian Captain

As Claudius exits, we hear a loud circus march, and Hamlet's father prances on pushing an office chair on castors. Hamlet follows. Both have black derbies which they hold high in the air. They circle the stage once, put on their derbies, and sit, Hamlet on the Ghost's lap.

THE VENTRILOQUIST'S DUMMY BIT

The Norwegian Captain enters up left and strides across the stage. Hamlet collapses into a dummy, crossing his eyes, with caved-in chest and wobbly neck. He speaks in an artificial dummy voice. The circus music fades. The Captain is in a hurry, but he is pulled back by each new question and his curiosity about the dummy.

HAMLET: Good sir, whose powers are these?

CAPTAIN: They are of Norway, sir.

GHOST: How purposed, sir, I pray you?

CAPTAIN: Against some part of Poland.

HAMLET: Who commands them, sir?

CAPTAIN: The nephew to old Fortinbras.

GHOST: Goes it against the main of Poland, sir, or for some frontier?

CAPTAIN: Truly to speak, and with no addition, we go to gain a little patch of ground that hath in it no profit but the name.

HAMLET: Why, then the Polack will never defend it, never defend it, never defend it.

CAPTAIN: Yes, it is already garrison'd.

GHOST: I humbly thank you, sir.

CAPTAIN: God be with you, sir.

SCENE XXVII: Hamlet and His Father Talk Things Over

Style note: This is the first in a series of scenes which are scarcely related by plot, and which are intended to create a total effect, rather than having any direct relation one to the other. Play each scene for its own values, and differentiate them sharply with music and lights.

At this point in the progress of the classical *Hamlet*, Hamlet leaves the stage for some five hundred lines. When he comes back he has changed, and whatever he has discovered off stage enables him to draw the play quickly to a close. Some sense of Hamlet's departure and his return, some sense of his trip, is what is intended here.

THE DUMMY BIT CONTINUES

HAMLET: How all occasions do inform against me
And spur my dull revenge!

GHOST: What is a man,
If the chief good and market of his time
Be but to sleep and feed?

HAMLET: A beast, no more.

GHOST: Sure, he that made us with such large discourse,
Looking before and after, gave us not
That capability and godlike reason
To fust in us unused.

HAMLET: Now, whether it be
Bestial oblivion,

GHOST: or some craven scruple

HAMLET: Of thinking too precisely on th' event—

GHOST: A thought which, quartered, hath but one part wisdom
   And ever three parts coward—

HAMLET: I do not know
   Why yet I live to say, 'This thing's to do,'
   Sith I have cause, and will, and strength,

GHOST: and means
   To do't.

HAMLET: Examples gross as earth exhort me.

GHOST: Witness this army of such mass and charge,
   Led by a delicate and tender prince,
   Whose spirit, with divine ambition puffed,
   Makes mouths at the invisible event,
   Exposing what is mortal and unsure
   To all that fortune, death, and danger dare,
   Even for an eggshell.

*The Ghost stands, easing Hamlet off his lap. Hamlet stands,
gradually losing his dummy voice and posture during the next
few speeches. The Ghost stands behind him on the chair.*

HAMLET [*removing his derby*]: Rightly to be great
   Is not to stir without great argument,

GHOST: But greatly to find quarrel in a straw
   When honour's at the stake.

HAMLET: How stand I then,
   That have a father killed,

GHOST: a mother stained,

HAMLET: Excitements of my reason and my blood,
   And let all sleep, while to my shame I see
   The imminent death of twenty thousand men

GHOST: That for a fantasy and trick of fame
   Go to their graves like beds,

HAMLET: fight for a plot
    Whereon the numbers cannot try the cause,
GHOST: Which is not tomb enough and continent
    To hide the slain?
HAMLET: O, from this time forth,
    My thoughts be bloody, or be nothing worth!

The circus music strikes up. Hamlet and the Ghost both remove their derbies and stand with their arms extended as if acknowledging great applause. The Ghost gets off the chair and prances out with it. Hamlet remains frozen with a fixed smile on his face, as the circus music fades and Rossencraft and Gilderstone enter.

SCENE XXVIII: Hamlet Gives Rossencraft and Gilderstone One Last Chance

ROSSENCRAFT: Will it please you go, my lord?

Hamlet goes to Gilderstone who is holding a cape for him. He still has the fixed smile on his face. Gilderstone puts the cape around Hamlet's shoulders and looks away. Hamlet goes to Rossencraft, who looks at him for a moment and then quickly ties the cape around him.

HAMLET: I'll be with you straight. Go before.

Rossencraft and Gilderstone exit, and we can see Gilderstone fumbling to get the gun out of his pocket. The circus music builds as Hamlet takes a gun from his pocket. He holds it aloft as he strides out after Rossencraft and Gilderstone. The circus music builds to crescendo and then stops abruptly. We hear two quick shots and then wild cheering fills the auditorium.

SCENE XXIX: Hamlet Justifies His Actions to the Multitude

Hamlet enters quickly carrying a microphone and acknowledging the wild applause. As he reaches center stage he is showered with confetti. The confetti and applause continue throughout the speech, and Hamlet must fight to be heard. His voice is carried over the loudspeaker system.

> *Suggestion*: Make the applause as loud as possible and reduce the volume only when Hamlet speaks, including several ear-splitting crescendos whenever Hamlet makes a point.

HAMLET: ROSSENCRAFT AND GILDERSTONE ARE DEAD! Why man, they did make love to their employment. They are not near my conscience. It is dangerous when the baser nature comes between the fell incensed points of mighty opposites. Does it not think *thee*, stand me now upon—he that hath killed my king, and whored my mother; popped in between the election and my hopes; thrown out his angle for my proper life—is't not perfect conscience to quit him with this arm? THE INTERIM IS MINE.

Hamlet places the microphone at the front of the stage, and as the applause and the shower of confetti reach a new peak of intensity, he exits, hands clenched over his head, acknowledging the applause. The applause suddenly stops and is succeeded immediately by a burst of vaudeville music.

SCENE XXX: The Fair Ophelia
Sings and Dances

A word of advice: This scene is an entertainment using vaudeville clichés and rock music. Play the scene as entertainment,
and do not try to indicate that Ophelia is mad.

*Ophelia, wearing black stockings and tails, dances on to the
vaudeville fanfare, making one tour of the stage, waving her
straw hat, and winking at the audience.*

The "Hamlet's Dead and Gone" Number

*The music switches to rock, and Ophelia cues the chorus with
a wave of her hat. The guards enter dancing in a chorus line,
swinging their nightsticks in unison. Three of the guards bear an
imaginary body above their heads. They sing:*

GUARDS: Hamlet's dead and gone, lady,
  Hamlet's dead and gone;
  At his head a grass-green turf;
  At his heels a stone.

The "How Should I
Your True Love Know" Number

*Ophelia picks up the microphone and begins a rock step in place
as she sings. Behind her, the guards also do a simple rock step
in unison. The three guards bearing the body set it down and
kneel solemnly.*

OPHELIA: How should I your true love know
  From another one?
  By his cockle hat and staff,
  And his sandal shoon.
  White his shroud as the mountain snow,
  Larded all with sweet flowers;
  Which bewept to the ground did not go
  With true love showers.

"HAMLET'S DEAD AND GONE, LADY" REPRISE

The three guards kneel again, picking up the body, and slowly march out the down-right tunnel, followed by the other guards who are also marching slowly and singing:

GUARDS: Hamlet's dead and gone, lady,
  Hamlet's dead and gone;
  At his head a grass-green turf;
  At his heels a stone.

THE VALENTINE'S DAY NUMBER
(*Ophelia, Polonius, Rossencraft, Gilderstone*)

The music changes to a more ballad-like rhythm and Ophelia cues Rossencraft, Gilderstone and Polonius who enter from the down-right tunnel. Rossencraft enters, carrying a red paper heart on a stick, and pulling a little red wagon in which sits Polonius who carries a pink lace parasol. Gilderstone, also carrying a heart, brings up the rear of the procession. All three wear simple smiles and wobble their heads as they move center stage. Ophelia takes Rossencraft's heart and puts her straw hat on his head. She will give the heart to someone in the audience during her song. She sings very sweetly, but on the last line she tosses her hair over her face and her voice becomes husky.

OPHELIA: Tomorrow is Saint Valentine's day,
  All in the morning betime,
  And I a maid at your window,
  To be your Valentine.
  Then up he rose and donn'd his clo'es,
  And dupp'd the chamber door;
  Let in the maid, that out a maid
  Never departed more.

The music stops for a moment, and Ophelia holds out the micro-phone to her father who speaks into it with a thin doll-voice.

POLONIUS: Tragical. Comical. Historical. Pastoral.

The Funeral March Number (*The Guards*)

The music strikes up again, now a jaunty rock number, and the chorus line of guards again crosses with a neat step. Ophelia takes her hat back from Rossencraft, and the three dolls exit as they came in. Ophelia waves good-bye. The guards sing:

GUARDS: They bore him bare-faced on the bier
  Hey non nonny, nonny, hey nonny
  And in his grave rained many a tear—
  Hey non nonny, nonny, hey nonny.

The "By Gis and By Saint Charity" Number (*Ophelia Solo*)

A powerful rock beat starts, and Ophelia sings straight to the audience. She is very sexy and tough, sometimes coy. She dances as she sings, at one point pulling aside her frock coat to show her ass, moving up to the circular staircase and rubbing up and down against it.

Note: Many people in their desire to think of Ophelia as a sweet young innocent, ignore how bawdy her songs are. Disillusion them. The first time she says "Cock," she does a bump, the second time she coyly covers the microphone, winks, and only hums the beat.

OPHELIA: By Gis and by Saint Charity,
Alack, and fie for shame!
Young men will do 't, if they come to 't;
By Cock they are to blame,
By Cock they are to blame.
Quoth she, before you tumbled me,
You promised me to wed.
So would I ha' done, by yonder sun,
And thou hadst not come to my bed,
And thou hadst not come to my bed.

THE "WILL A' NOT" NUMBER
(*Ophelia and Ramon*)

The music picks up a new, slower song, as Ophelia sees Hamlet enter. He is dressed as Ramon and pushes a wire litter basket strapped to a dolly. As she sings, Ophelia takes the heart away from the person she gave it to before, and sweetly hands it to someone else. She then goes to Ramon who picks her up and puts her in the basket. Ramon points a gun at her head. Ophelia pulls the trigger. It fires, her head slumps, and she slowly sings the last line.

OPHELIA: And will a' not come again?
And will a' not come again?
He is gone, he is gone,
And we cast away moan,
God ha' mercy on his soul!
And of all Christian souls, I pray God,
God be wi' you.

The vaudeville play-off music strikes up and Ramon pushes Ophelia off in the litter basket. She revives and waves her hat gaily to the audience as they exit. The play-off music dies, the stage lights dim, and the Ghost enters, wearing a frock coat and top hat and carrying a bunch of purple flowers.

SCENE XXXI: Ramon Meets a Tourist

The Ghost clears his throat and sings a cappella *in a deep, rich voice of which he is obviously very proud.*

GHOST: In youth, when I did love, did love;
  Me thought 'twas very sweet,
  To contract the time for my behove,
  O methought there was nothing meet.

THE HIGH-BROW LOW-LIFE BIT

(a) As the Ghost begins the second verse of his song, Ramon enters, humming to himself and pushing the litter basket which now has a cover on it. (b) The Ghost gives him a disparaging look, but continues singing. (c) Ramon climbs up on the litter basket and sits there, still humming. (d) The Ghost gives him a disparaging look but continues singing. (e) Ramon pops open a beer which he has concealed in a paper bag and begins to drink. The beer sprays all over the Ghost. (f) At the end of the second verse, the Ghost finally has to stop singing and confront the ruffian.

GHOST [*continues singing*]: But age with his stealing steps,
  Hath clawed me in his clutch,
  And hath shipped me into the land,
  As if I never had been such.

The Ghost nods confidently to the audience and proceeds to deal with the young man who has interrupted his act.

The Low-Brow High-Life Bit
with Spanish Innuendo

Ramon speaks with a heavy Puerto Rican accent, and it seems the Ghost, too, knows a little Spanish which he displays proudly. As the scene continues, the Ghost becomes angrier and angrier and attempts more and more to control his temper.

> *A note of perhaps historical interest only*: For a while the scene was played with Hamlet speaking entirely in Spanish, and with the Ghost translating for the audience's benefit. This is an amusing device for a while but it obscures the action of the scene and also many of the jokes.
>
> *A more important note*: You should not make any reference in the scene to the father-son relationship or to the Ghost-Hamlet relationship, as these will only obscure the scene.

GHOST: Whose grave's this?

HAMLET: Mine, señor.

GHOST: I think it be thine indeed, for thou liest in 't.

HAMLET: You lie out on 't, señor, and therefore 't is not yours. For my part, I do not lie in 't, yet it is mine.

GHOST: Thou dost lie in 't, to be in 't and say it is thine. 'Tis for the dead, not for the quick. Therefore thou liest.

HAMLET: 'Tis a quick lie, señor. 'Twill away again from me to you.

GHOST: What hombre dost thou dig it for?

HAMLET: For no man, señor.

GHOST: What señorita, then?

HAMLET: For none, neither.

GHOST: Who is to be buried in it?

HAMLET: One that was a woman, señor; but, rest her soul, she's dead.

GHOST: Tell me, paisano. How long hast thou been a grave-maker?

HAMLET: Of all the days in the year, I came to it that day that our last King Hamlet overcame Fortinbras.

GHOST: How long is that since?

HAMLET: Cannot you tell that? Every fool can tell that. It was that very day that young Hamlet was born—he that is mad and sent to Washington.

GHOST: Why was he sent into Washington?

HAMLET: Why, because he was mad. He shall recover his wits there; or if he do not, 'tis no great matter there.

GHOST: Porque?

HAMLET: 'Twill not be seen in him there. There the mens are as mad as he is.

GHOST: How came he loco?

HAMLET: Very strangely, they say.

GHOST: How, peculiario?

HAMLET: Faith, e'en with losing his wits.

GHOST: Upon what ground?

The Capper

Hamlet leaps off the litter basket, removing the cover and throwing the now empty beer can into it. Then he and the Ghost raise their hands in a vaudeville salute and speak in chorus.

HAMLET and GHOST: Why here, insanity!

The vaudeville play-off music strikes up and the Ghost with a wave, runs off, pushing the litter basket. Hamlet runs up the circular staircase, tossing the lid of the litter basket down onto the stage from the first level, then climbing the ladder to his perch.

SCENE XXXII: Ramon Speaks His Mind: Hamlet Is Still Alone (III)

Hamlet arrives at the top level out of breath. He immediately picks up a microphone and begins speaking, still with his Puerto Rican accent.

HAMLET: To be or not to be, that is the question:
  Whether 'tis nobler in the mind to suffer
  The slings and arrows of outrageous fortune,
  Or to take arms against a sea of troubles
  And by opposing end them. To die: to sleep.
  No more! and by a sleep to say we end
  The heart-ache and the thousand natural shocks
  That flesh is heir to: 'tis a consummation
  Devoutly to be wish'd. To die: to sleep.
  To sleep? perchance to dream! Ay, there's the rub;
  For in that sleep of death what dreams may come,
  When we have shuffled off this mortal coil,
  Must give us pause.

> *Note*: The audience will probably find Ramon's rendering of this, most famous of all speeches, very funny, but by now their laughter will have begun to subside. Hamlet, too, changes, removing his wig and speaking more carefully, but still with his accent. The audience will become very quiet.

                    There's the respect
  That makes calamity of so long life;
  For who would bear the whips and scorns of time,
  Th' oppressor's wrong, the proud man's contumely,
  The pangs of dispriz'd love, the law's delay,

The insolence of office, and the spurns
That patient merit of th' unworthy takes,
When he himself might his quietus make
With a bare bodkin? Who would fardels bear,
To grunt and sweat under a weary life,
But that the dread of something after death,
The undiscover'd country from whose bourn
No traveller returns, puzzles the will,
And makes us rather bear those ills we have
Than fly to others that we know not of?

THE GATHERING STORM

*A clock begins ticking, slowly and sharply. The sliding doors
open: Claudius, Gertrude, Laertes, and Claudius' bodyguard walk
out onto the dark stage. Laertes is held firmly by the guard.
Horatio enters at the back of the house and stands on one of the
railings in the audience, his back against a pillar. On the first
level of catwalks, the guards appear and stand quietly, facing
the audience. They are wearing sweatshirts instead of their
normal fatigue shirts and are without their helmets and sunglasses. Hamlet observes this movement and then resumes
speaking.*

Thus conscience does make cowards of us all,
And thus the native hue of resolution
Is sicklied o'er with the pale cast of thought,
And enterprises of great pitch and moment
With this regard their currents turn awry,
And lose the name of action.

*On the word "action," the lights come up full on stage, the
ticking ceases, and the guards begin a rhythmic clapping.*

SCENE XXXIII: Everyone Dies

Dress, for this final scene, is formal: Claudius is wearing his dress blues, Gertrude her evening gown, while Laertes is wearing a heavy coat over a corduroy suit. The words and action are crisp and business-like; only Hamlet works to disrupt the scene. He continues to speak in his Puerto Rican accent as the other characters try to ignore him. The bodyguard holds Laertes firmly until Claudius orders him to release the boy.

THE HIGH-DRAMA LOW-COMEDY BIT

LAERTES: O thou vile king, give me my father!

HAMLET: Calmly, good Laertes.

CLAUDIUS: Let him go. Tell me, Laertes, why thou art thus incens'd? Let him go. Speak, man.

LAERTES: Where is my father?

CLAUDIUS: Dead.

HAMLET: But not by him.

LAERTES: How came he dead? I'll not be juggled with! To hell, allegiance! I'll be revenged for my father.

CLAUDIUS: Who shall stay you? Good Laertes, that I am guiltless of your father's death, and am most sensibly in grief for it, it shall as level to your judgement 'pear as day does to your eye.

LAERTES: Where is my sister?

HAMLET: Over there, Laertes, in the manhole.

Hamlet is referring to the lid of the litter basket which is still lying center stage.

The Sentimental Moment (Part I)

The guards stop their rhythmic clapping as Laertes kneels and lifts the cover. He replaces it quickly.

LAERTES: O heat, dry up my brains! O rose of May, dear maid, kind sister, sweet Ophelia! Do you see this, O God? And so have I a noble father and a beauteous sister lost, a sister whose worth, if praises may go back again, stood challenger-on-mount of all the age for her perfections. But my revenge will come.

The guards resume clapping, as Laertes stands.

CLAUDIUS: Break not your sleeps for that. You must not think that we are made of stuff so flat and dull that we can let our beard be shook with danger and think it pastime. You shortly shall hear more. I lov'd your father and your sister as we love ourself.

The Sentimental Moment (Part II)

Gertrude comes forward and picks up the lid of Ophelia's grave. She places a flower under the lid and then sets it down again.

GERTRUDE: Farewell! I hop'd thou shouldst have been my Hamlet's wife. I thought thy bride-bed to have deck'd, sweet maid, and not have strew'd thy grave.

CLAUDIUS: Hamlet slew thy father and thy sister. What would you undertake to show yourself in deed your father's son more than in words?

LAERTES: To cut his throat i' th' church.

The Great Revelation

The guards cease clapping as Hamlet, stripping off the last of his Ramon clothes, stands on the third level and speaks in his normal voice.

HAMLET: What is he whose grief bears such an emphasis? This is I, Hamlet the Dane.

The guards turn around revealing "HAMLET THE DANE" emblazoned on the back of each of their sweatshirts. They resume the clapping, while they jog in place and flex their muscles as if preparing for a fight.

LAERTES: The devil take thy soul!
HAMLET [*begins to climb down the ladder from the third level*]: Hear you, sir. What is the reason that you use me thus? I loved you ever, but it is no matter. Let Hercules himself do what he may, the cat will mew and the dog will have his day.

Laertes flings off his overcoat and starts to run up the circular staircase. He is stopped by Claudius' words.

CLAUDIUS: Will you be ruled by me?
LAERTES: Ay, my lord. So you will not o'errule me to a peace. [*He jumps down from the circular staircase and moves to Claudius.*]
CLAUDIUS: To thine own peace. Osric, the pistol.

Osric exits up stage. While Claudius speaks, Hamlet says good-bye to each guard in turn, taking a slap on the hand from each in time with the clapping. Hamlet then climbs down the circular staircase and stands while his cape is thrown over his shoulders by Claudius' bodyguard; he is also wearing his beret and glasses. He then moves into the audience and stands with Horatio.

CLAUDIUS [*to audience*]: I will work him to an exploit now ripe in my device, under the which he shall not choose but fall. And for his death no wind of blame shall breathe but even his own mother shall uncharge the practice and call it accident.

> *Note*: There is no attempt at secrecy here; Claudius speaks openly, even nodding to Gertrude when he mentions her. The scene is not a series of conspiracies, but a public ceremony.

LAERTES: My lord, I will be ruled. The rather if you could devise it so that I might be the organ.

Osric re-enters and hands a revolver to Claudius.

CLAUDIUS: It falls right. Osric!

Claudius motions for Osric to address Hamlet, and Osric crosses the stage to speak to the young prince from the foot of the steps leading into the audience. While he and Hamlet speak, Laertes lights a cigarette and paces the stage.

OSRIC: Your lordship is right welcome back to Denmark.

HAMLET: I humbly thank you, sir.

OSRIC: Sweet lord, if your lordship were at leisure, I should impart a thing to you from his majesty.

HAMLET: I will receive it, sir, with all diligence of spirit.

OSRIC: It would come to immediate trial if your lordship would vouchsafe the answer.

A DOUBLE TAKE

HAMLET: How if I answer no?

The guards stop clapping; everyone looks at Hamlet.

> *Theoretical note*: Here again Hamlet seems to break the form of the play itself. At one point in rehearsal, Hamlet was still on the third level, and one of the guards climbed up and twisted his arm until he agreed to go on with the play. We found this move to be too extended and forced, as well as being a rehash of the fight scene. A simple pause here will serve.

OSRIC: Sir?

HAMLET [*laughs, then answers*]: If it please his majesty, it is the breathing time of day with me. Let the pistol be brought, the gentleman willing, and the king hold his purpose.

The guards resume clapping.

OSRIC: Shall I deliver you so?

HAMLET: To this effect, sir, after what flourish your nature will.

OSRIC: I commend my duty to your lordship.

HAMLET: Yours, yours.

A WORD OF CAUTION TO BUILD SUSPENSE

HORATIO: You will lose this duel, my lord.

HAMLET: I do not think so. I have been in continual practice. I shall win, but thou wouldst not think how ill all's here about my heart. But it is no matter.

HORATIO: If your mind dislike anything, obey it. I will say you are not fit.

HAMLET: Not a whit, we defy augury.

Hamlet and Horatio walk to the stage, where Claudius and Laertes are standing center.

THE GAME IS SET UP

HAMLET: Give us the pistols.

CLAUDIUS [*points the gun at the floor and pulls the trigger—it clicks six times*]: Six. You know the game Hamlet?

HAMLET: Very well, my lord.

CLAUDIUS: [*takes a bullet from Osric and inserts it in the gun*]: One. [*He closes the chamber and spins it.*]

HAMLET [*to Horatio, showing him a line in the text he is carrying*]: A man's life is no more than to say "One."

THE CROSS-UP

Claudius holds out the gun to Hamlet but, when he reaches for it, places it in Laertes' hand. Laertes stubs out his cigarette and moves down left.

CLAUDIUS: Come begin.

HAMLET: Come on, sir. [*He is now standing by the circular staircase, diagonally across the stage from Laertes.*]

ROUND ONE

Horatio moves in front of Hamlet and hands him a black blindfold, which Hamlet ties over Horatio's eyes. The clapping stops. Laertes aims and pulls the trigger. BANG! Horatio collapses as Hamlet grasps him from behind and eases his fall to the stage. The clock resumes ticking. Laertes comes forward with the gun which he gives to Hamlet, and stands staring at Horatio while Hamlet opens the gun, extracts the spent shell, and reloads with a new bullet which he takes from Osric. Hamlet spins the chamber and hands the gun to Laertes.

ROUND TWO

HAMLET: I'll be your target, Laertes. In mine ignorance your skill shall like a star in the darkest night, stick fiery off indeed.

Laertes takes the gun. Hamlet moves down left.

LAERTES: You mock me, sir.

HAMLET: No, by this hand.

Hamlet, one hand in the air, turns and faces Laertes who is now standing by the circular staircase. Hamlet closes his eyes and cringes as Laertes pulls the trigger. CLICK. Hamlet smiles and crosses the stage to get the gun. As Hamlet moves back to his place with the gun, Laertes glares at Claudius, who shrugs. Laertes then stands rigidly by the staircase as Hamlet turns and quickly fires. BANG! Laertes gasps and grabs his stomach. Hamlet quickly opens the gun and removes the spent cartridge. He looks up and sees that Laertes has not fallen.

A PALPABLE ABSURDITY

HAMLET: One.

LAERTES [*protesting*]: No.

HAMLET [*to Claudius*]: Judgement.

CLAUDIUS [*looks at Laertes*]: A hit, a very palpable hit.

Laertes falls, clutching the staircase.

THE GAME MOVES INTO EXTRA INNINGS

Hamlet crosses to Osric, who is standing up center, and takes another bullet.

> *Note*: Do not involve yourself with questions, such as why does Osric have extra bullets, or corollary debates about why Gertrude allows all this to happen. Remember that the scene is a matter-of-fact ceremony or game, that the results are contained in the text to which Hamlet occasionally refers, and that the audience will only become confused if you attempt to touch on every behavioral detail at this climactic point. The scene should have an inexorable movement to it (aided by the clapping of the guards or the ticking clock) and should admit of no questions.

Hamlet reloads the gun and spins the chamber as he looks around at the remaining contestants with a smile. He moves toward his mother who backs away and finally holds out the gun to Claudius who takes it confidently. When Claudius takes the gun, the ticking stops and there is silence.

HAMLET: Come, my lord, you do but dally; I pray you.

ROUND THREE

Hamlet crosses down right to his mother who hands him a blindfold and stands in front of her son with her arms reaching out for Claudius. Hamlet ties the blindfold on her as Claudius fires from the hip. BANG! *Gertrude gives a little cry and falls. Hamlet says a short silent prayer over his mother and takes the gun from Claudius, who is unmoved. Hamlet takes another bullet from Osric, reloads, spins the chamber, and moves down right.*

THE EXECUTIVE MOTIF

As Hamlet crosses down right, the guards above, Claudius' bodyguard, and Osric all put on blindfolds. Hamlet aims at Claudius and fires. CLICK. *Hamlet is perplexed. Claudius smiles as Hamlet crosses to give him the gun. Hamlet goes back to his place, giving the audience a worried look. He turns to face Claudius and the king fires.* CLICK.

FOUL PLAY ·

Hamlet gives a big sigh of relief, and smiles at the audience as he goes to get the gun. Suddenly Claudius fires again. CLICK. *Angry, Claudius fires again and again.* CLICK. CLICK. CLICK. CLICK. CLICK. CLICK. *Claudius looks at the gun in amazement as Hamlet takes it from him.*

HAMLET: A man's life is no more than to say *"One,"* my lord.

THE COUP DE GRACE

Claudius refuses to believe that the game will go on but he and Hamlet exchange places. Hamlet moves behind Claudius' bodyguard, holds the guard's arm out at full length, and rests the gun on it as he aims at Claudius. He fires. BANG!

THE FOUR-PART CATACLYSM

No one moves. Claudius is astounded that the gun went off.
   (1) The bodyguard falls. (Laugh.)

(2) Osric falls. (Laugh.)

(3) All the guards above fall. (Big Laugh.)

(4) Claudius stares in disbelief at the carnage around him, refusing to believe that he has been shot. Hamlet takes out the text and points out to the King that he indeed dies. Claudius throws down his hat in disgust and lies down.

THE ATTEMPTED SUICIDE

Hamlet now reloads, taking a bullet from Osric's hand. He kneels center stage among the bodies, nods good-bye to the audience, takes a deep breath, and points the gun at his head.

ONE LAST GAG

Hamlet holds this position until someone in the audience giggles or coughs. He looks up in disgust and lowers the gun.

THE FALSE ENDING

Hamlet smiles and offers the gun to someone in the audience. Someone accepts and Hamlet leads him onto the stage.

> *Sociological note*: Someone will always accept the role of Hamlet's murderer. But Hamlet should make sure to choose a man, since women occasionally declined actually to pull the trigger, forcing Hamlet to get someone else, which put an unwanted pause in the action.

Hamlet stations the person on one side of the stage, and then says a few last words.

HAMLET: There is a special providence in the fall of a sparrow. If it be now, 'tis not to come; if it be not to come, it will be now; if it be not now, yet it will come: the readiness is all.

Hamlet spreads his arms to present a good target. The man pulls the trigger. CLICK. *Immediately there is loud cheering and clapping over the loudspeakers, as Hamlet retrieves the gun and escorts the man back to his seat.*

THE BANANA PEEL BIT

Hamlet gestures for quiet and the cheering recedes slightly. He speaks triumphantly.

You that look pale and tremble at this chance, that are but mutes of audience to this act, had I but time, O I could tell you . . .

Hamlet throws away the text, and waving to the audience starts to run up the circular staircase. He trips and the gun goes off. BANG! The cheering stops. Hamlet staggers back on stage, picks up the book, and reads from it.

The rest is silence.

He falls and the lights go out as the cheering resumes.

THE CURTAIN CALL

Hamlet has exited in the black-out.

The lights come up and the loud rock music starts again. The Ghost, Rossencraft, Gilderstone, and Polonius enter as the whole company stands and sings a chorus of "Hamlet's Dead and Gone, Lady." Claudius picks up the text which Hamlet dropped, and he walks off reading it as everyone else runs off with the vaudeville play-off music.

Hamlet enters dancing, takes a bow and signals the rest of the company to come back on for another bow. Everyone runs on again and they take a company bow to each side of the house.

Claudius is still absorbed with the book and he goes up to Hamlet and starts arguing with him, as he is trying to take his bows.

As the rest of the company exits, Claudius and Hamlet start pushing each other, and end up wrestling on the floor. Finally Hamlet escapes and Claudius chases him off stage as two guards enter through the sliding doors. They are carrying a huge funeral wreath with a picture of Hamlet on one side, and on the other "R.I.P. Will Shakespeare." After showing the wreath to all sides of the house they place it against the circular staircase and exit.

The houselights come on and the music fades but keeps playing until audience has left.

APPENDIX

THE SONGS

composed and arranged by Galt MacDermot

SCENE XVII
  "Woe Is Me," sung by Hamlet and Ophelia, accompanied by
  Horatio on guitar.
  "Why, Let the Stricken Deer Go Weep," sung by Hamlet at the
  end of the scene, no accompaniment.

SCENE XXX (*following songs done with full rock accompaniment*)
  "Hamlet's Dead and Gone, Lady," sung by the Guards
  "How Should I Your True Love Know," sung by Ophelia
  "Tomorrow Is Saint Valentine's Day," sung by Ophelia
  "By Gis and By Saint Charity," sung by Ophelia
  "An' Will A' Not Come Again," sung by Ophelia

SCENE XXXI
  "In Youth," sung *a cappella* by the Ghost to introduce the scene

Woe Is Me

(*Ophelia and Hamlet*)

(*Ophelia*) Woe is me. You are so sick of late.

So far from cheer and from your for - mer state.

(*Hamlet*) I must leave thee, love, and short-ly too.

My operant powers their functions leave to do,

And thou shalt live in this fair world be - hind,

Honored, be - loved and hap-ly one as kind ___

For husband shalt thou— (*Ophelia*) O confound the rest!

Such love must needs be trea-son in my breast.

In sec-ond hus - band let me be ac-curst;

None wed the sec - ond but who killed the first. ___

A sec-ond time I kill my husband dead,

When sec-ond hus - band kiss-es me in bed.

Both here and hence pur - sue me last-ing strife,

If once a wid - ow, ev-er I be wife. ___

Why, Let the Stricken Deer Go Weep

(Hamlet)

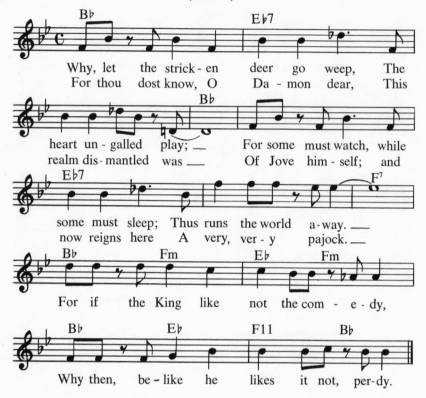

Why, let the strick-en deer go weep, The
For thou dost know, O Da-mon dear, This

heart un-galled play; — For some must watch, while
realm dis-mantled was — Of Jove him-self; and

some must sleep; Thus runs the world a-way. —
now reigns here A very, ver-y pajock. —

For if the King like not the com-e-dy,

Why then, be-like he likes it not, per-dy.

Hamlet's Dead and Gone

(Guards)

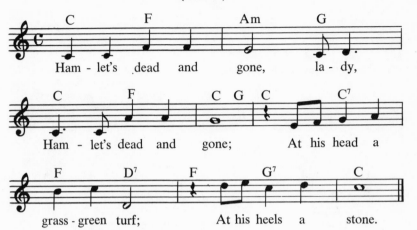

Ham - let's dead and gone, la - dy,

Ham - let's dead and gone; At his head a

grass - green turf; At his heels a stone.

How Should I Your True Love Know?
(*Ophelia*)

How should I your true love know From an-oth-er one? By his cock - le hat and staff, And his san-dal shoon.

White his shroud as the moun - tain snow, Lard-ed all with sweet flowers; ____ Which be-wept to the ground did not go With true love showers. ____

Tomorrow Is St. Valentine's Day

(Ophelia)

To - mor-row is Saint Val- en-tine's day, —

All in the morn-ing be - time _____

And I a maid at your win - dow _____

To be your Val - - en - tine.

Then up he rose and donn'd his clo'es,

And dupp'd the cham - ber door; _____

Let in the maid, that out a mai - - d

Nev - er de - part - - ed more.

By Gis and by Saint Charity

(Ophelia)

By Gis and by Saint Char - i - ty, A -
lack, and fie for shame! Young
men will do't, if they come to't; By
Cock they are to bla - me. By
Cock they are to blame.
Quoth she, be - fore you tum - bled me, You
prom - ised me to wed. So
would I ha' done, by yon - der sun, An thou

hadst not come to my bed, An thou

hadst ___ not come to my bed.

And Will A' Not Come Again?

(Ophelia)

And will a' not come a - gain?

And will a' not come a - gain? He is

gone, he is gone, And we cast a-way mo- an, _

God ha' mer- cy on his soul! ____ And of all

Chris-tian souls, I pray God, God be wi' you.

In Youth

(*Ghost*)

In youth, when I did love, did love: ___
age with his steal - ing steps, ___

Me - thought it was ve - ry
Hath clawed me in his

sweet, To con-tract the time for my be - hove, __
clutch, And hath shipped me in - to the land, __

Oh me-thought there was noth - ing meet,
As if I nev - er had been such,

there was noth - ing meet. _____
nev - er had been such. _____

But

THE SOURCES

SCENE I: BY WAY OF A PROLOGUE

The guards' lines are taken from the exchange between Bernardo and Francisco, which are the first lines of the standard edition (I, i, 1–5).

The next sequence has very complicated roots. It is built around the first exchange between Hamlet and Horatio in the standard text (I, ii, 159–188), which is here cut and slightly amended to exclude Marcellus and Bernardo.

When Hamlet talks about *Hamlet*, he uses lines from (II, ii, 456–466), Polonius' introduction of the players to Hamlet. The following derogatory remarks are from the same scene, line 521.

The speech which Hamlet and Horatio read from the text is spoken by Hamlet on the battlements while he and Horatio are waiting for the appearance of the Ghost (I, iv, 23–36). The speech is slightly shortened here.

The last line of the scene is from (III, ii, 94–96), spoken to Horatio immediately before the play within the play. Here, as throughout the text, pronouns are often changed to fit the new situation (*I* becomes *we* here).

SCENE II: CLAUDIUS TELLS EVERYONE WHAT IS HAPPENING

This scene retains the same shape as in the standard version (I, ii, 1–63), but it has been considerably cut. Osric here takes the place of Cornelius and Voltemand. "The Stupid Guard Bit" is composed of actors' adlibs. Laertes' interruption of Claudius is also original here.

SCENE III: THE FAMILY TALKS THINGS OVER

In the same shape as the standard version but with cuts (I, ii, 64–128).

SCENE IV: HAMLET IS STILL ALONE

This scene is Hamlet's first soliloquy (I, ii, 135–159) which begins "O that this too, too solid flesh would melt." The first six lines have been cut.

SCENE V: A TRAVELER RETURNS

Essentially the same scene as in the standard text (I, v, 1–106), but considerably cut, principally in the Ghost's description of the manner of his death. Here also the Ghost says that he has been burned to death rather than poisoned, and that the story given out was that he was struck by lightning rather than stung by a serpent. The line "Angels and ministers of grace, defend us!" is taken from the moment in the standard text when Hamlet first sees the Ghost (I, iv, 39).

SCENE VI: THE TWO FRIENDS MEET AGAIN BUT HAMLET HAS CHANGED

In the standard version (I, v, 117–137) the situation is the same, but Marcellus is also in the scene. Some lines are considerably altered, and the ending is abridged past recognition. The Ghost is no longer under the ground and he is no longer seeking to make them swear the oath. The lines "Good night, Horatio" and "Good night, my lord" are new.

SCENE VII: A FEW PRECEPTS

Taken from Polonius' all too famous last bit of advice to Laertes and somewhat abridged in itself (I, iii, 58–80).

SCENE VIII: THE SHORTEST SCENE IN THE PLAY

The line (III, i, 89–90) occurs in the standard text at the end of the "To be or not to be" soliloquy, and introduces the scene in which Hamlet rants at Ophelia.

SCENE IX: POLONIUS LAYS DOWN THE LAW

This scene is an amalgam of two scenes from the standard text (II, i, 74–108, and I, iv, 98–135), used here in reverse order and abridged to remove any references to the King's involvement in the scheme. There are other small changes to bring the scene in line with the stage situation, and specific references to Polonius' hiding is also struck.

Hamlet's line, "Intermission! Houselights!" is, of course, original.

SCENE X: THE PEANUT SCENE

The same scene as in the standard text (III, ii, 93–157) but for one or two words and the addition of Hamlet's peanut-selling lines. Ophelia's comment on what she has seen (which she makes after Hamlet exits in the standard text) is here eliminated because Hamlet drives her from the stage.

SCENE XI: THE PEANUT SCENE REPRISE

In the classical version this is Hamlet's first "mad scene" (II, ii, 170–221). It is abridged here, eliminating one or two of Hamlet's jokes and some of Polonius' interpretive asides.

SCENE XII: CLAUDIUS AND GERTRUDE WELCOME TWO OLD FRIENDS OF HAMLET TO THE PALACE

This scene is taken directly from the standard text (II, ii, 1–34) except for one or two word changes and the lengthy Ramon interpolation which was ad-libbed. The names Rossencraft and Gilderstone are from the 1603 quarto.

SCENE XIII: HAMLET WELCOMES HIS TWO OLD FRIENDS TO DENMARK

Almost word for word, the same as in the standard text (II, ii, 226–398), except for one or two minor cuts for reasons of clarity and the elimination of the long discussion of the players. Hamlet's last line is original.

SCENE XIV: FATHER AND SON HAVE AN IDEA

The lines which Hamlet and the Ghost share are taken from the end of Hamlet's soliloquy "O what a rogue and peasant slave am I" (III, i, 616–623 and 632–633).

SCENE XV: CLAUDIUS IS CONCERNED ABOUT HAMLET

The same as in the standard text (III, i, 1–28) except for minor word changes and the elimination of reference to the players.

SCENE XVI: GETTING READY FOR THE PARTY

The same as in the standard text (III, ii, 59–79), but somewhat abridged to eliminate Hamlet's instructions to Horatio about watching the King. Horatio's line, "At your service, my lord," is an adlib.

SCENE XVII: CLAUDIUS IS HUMILIATED AT HAMLET'S PARTY

This scene follows the pattern of Act III, scene ii, in the standard text, but in addition to the actual textual changes which center around the elimination of the players, many of the old words have entirely new references and imply actions entirely foreign to classical interpretations. To get the sense of the new uses to which the old words are put, you must, of course, refer to the text itself.

There is also in the scene additional material taken from other scenes in the standard version and some few original lines.

The welcoming of Polonius, Ophelia, Rossencraft, and Gilderstone is taken from (III, ii, 51–56), but the lines specifically to Ophelia are original here. The by-play with Polonius is from (III, ii, 105–111) with Polonius's answer about "tragical, comical . . ." interpolated from (II, ii, 415–418) where he tells Hamlet that the players have arrived at the castle. It is they whom he calls the best actors in the world, not himself, as in this text. All this by-play in the standard text takes place after the King and Queen's entrance (III, ii, 96–103), but in our version the party gradually gathers and is not in full swing until the King has arrived and been included in the festivities. The next sequence follows the standard text (III, ii, 113–164) up to the beginning of the play-within-the-play itself, eliminating only the dumb show and with few changes. Hamlet himself speaks the prologue, and again the sense of many lines is changed by the action that accompanies them.

Hamlet's request for Ophelia to sing is, of course, original. The lyrics for her song and Hamlet's are taken from the lines of the Player King and Player Queen (III, ii, 173–174, 183–190, 194–195, 232–233).

The sequence of lines immediately after Ophelia's song follow, in the standard version, immediately after the Player King goes to sleep in the play-within-the-play (III, ii, 239–262). There are here some word changes which reflect the somewhat different situation in this version.

Hamlet's line, "Ha, ha boy! Art thou there, true-penny!" is in the standard text, spoken by Hamlet to the Ghost (I, v, 49) as the Old Mole moves about under the stage. Hamlet's line, "Madam, I pray you," is original, and her line is the Player Queen's last line when she sees her husband asleep (III, ii, 238–239).

Claudius' speech is from the Ghost's revelation to Hamlet at their first encounter (I, v, 47–52, 56–57, 74–75) with one or two word changes to make the cuts work grammatically.

Hamlet's taunting of Claudius is, of course, a soliloquy in the standard text which he speaks much before the play-within-the-play (II, ii, 575–608). Some of the lines in the soliloquy as it is presented in the standard text were used to make Scene XIV in our version, and the speech is further cut here to eliminate specific references to the players.

SCENE XVIII: HAMLET SAVORS HIS TRIUMPH

This scene is the same shape as the standard text and occurs at the same relative position (III, ii, 282–405). Hamlet's conversation with Horatio is now simply a song, the interruption of the players is eliminated, and there are some small word changes. Here Hamlet says good-night to Horatio separately and these lines are original.

SCENE XIX: HAMLET IS STILL ALONE (II)

These few lines follow immediately in the standard text (III, ii, 406–410).

SCENE XX: OSRIC REPORTS FROM NORWAY WHILE ROSSENCRAFT AND GILDERSTONE FIND OUT WHAT LIFE IS REALLY LIKE

This scene is the amalgamation of two scenes from the standard text. The lines between Claudius and Osric are from the exchange between Claudius and Cornelius and Voltemand (II, ii, 59–79). Claudius' lines to Rossencraft and Gilderstone are found in (III, iii, 1–25) in the standard text. In the standard text Rosencrantz and Guildenstern are willing helpers in the King's plan but they do not know that it includes murder.

SCENE XXI: HAMLET KILLS POLONIUS AND DRIVES HIS MOTHER CRAZY

This scene retains the same shape as the standard version (III, iv, 1–217), but there are substantial cuts which materially affect the sense of the scene. Polonius' death is here passed over even more superficially than in the classical text, Hamlet's tirades are shortened, and his explanations to his mother about whether he is mad or not are eliminated. The apparent reconciliation of Hamlet and his mother is also weakened.

Hamlet's description of Claudius, "Like a mildew'd ear," is found in the 1603 Quarto (III, iv, 38–40).

Here the Ghost remains until the end of the scene, usurps two of Hamlet's lines, and is the object of some lines which, in the classical text, Hamlet addresses to his mother.

SCENE XXII: CLAUDIUS IN PURSUIT OF HAMLET

It is implied in the standard text that this scene occurs later and at a different place than the confrontation between Hamlet and Gertrude, but we again retain the same shape as the standard text (IV, i, 1–45) with major cuts which speed the scene but do not alter the sense.

SCENE XXIII: THE CHASE

The same words as the standard text (IV, ii, 1–30) with but one or two word changes.

SCENE XXIV: THE INTERROGATION

What we have eliminated in this entire section of the play, are
Claudius' private moments in which he often reveals his more human,
or sometimes more cunning, thoughts. Here we see him only in
action.

In this particular scene we have eliminated a brief private specula-
tion by the King and short conversation with Rossencraft and Gilderstone, and proceeded directly to the interrogation which follows as
in the standard text with only minor word changes (IV, iii, 17–57).

SCENE XXV: CLAUDIUS SHOWS HIS
TRUE NATURE

The conversation with the Captain is original in this text. Claudius'
few lines after the Captain's exit are taken from the end of the
scene in the standard text which is the source of Scene XXIV (IV,
iii, 65–69).

SCENE XXVI: HAMLET AND HIS FATHER
HAVE A CONVERSATION WITH THE
NORWEGIAN CAPTAIN

There are some abridgements in the scene and some of Hamlet's
lines are given to the Ghost (IV, iv, 9–29). Fortinbras introduces
the scene in the standard text.

SCENE XXVII: HAMLET AND HIS FATHER
TALK THINGS OVER

In the standard text (IV, iv, 32–66) this conversation is Hamlet's
soliloquy which he speaks immediately after encountering the Captain. We have here simply given the Ghost some of the lines, and
the words are themselves the same.

SCENE XXVIII: HAMLET GIVES ROSSENCRAFT
AND GILDERSTONE ONE LAST CHANCE

The lines used here occur in the standard text immediately before
the "How all occasions do inform against me" soliloquy (IV, iv, 30–
31), and carry none of the implications which they are asked to bear
here.

SCENE XXIX: HAMLET JUSTIFIES HIMSELF TO THE MULTITUDES

At this point in our text the sequence of scenes is drastically altered from what has come to be considered standard.

This speech is compiled largely of lines which Hamlet delivers to Horatio following the scene in which Hamlet jumped into Ophelia's grave. In the standard text he is explaining the circumstances of his escape and discovery of Claudius' plot against him (V, ii, 57–73).

The first line of the speech is most often spoken by an ambassador to Fortinbras after all the principals are dead (V, ii, 382).

SCENE XXX: THE FAIR OPHELIA

All the songs are, in the standard text, sung in madness by Ophelia in the presence of Gertrude, Claudius, or Laertes. A great deal of weeping and plotting surrounds them (IV, v).

SCENE XXXI: RAMON MEETS A TOURIST

The Ghost's song is in the standard text sung by one of the grave-diggers (V, i, 69–72, 79–82).

The scene between the Ghost and Ramon occurs in the standard text between Hamlet and the Gravedigger (V, i, 126–176). Ramon is given the Gravedigger's lines, and the Ghost speaks Hamlet's lines. There are some small cuts, one or two word changes, and, of course, all the Spanish interpolations are original.

SCENE XXXII: HAMLET IS STILL ALONE (III) OR RAMON SPEAKS HIS MIND

Unchanged from (III, i, 56–87).

SCENE XXXIII: EVERYONE DIES

This scene has extraordinarily complicated roots in the standard text and is essentially a new scene composed out of pieces from the old text.

You will find the pieces in the following scenes:

Laertes' return to Denmark and confrontation of Claudius (IV, v). Hamlet as Ramon takes some of Gertrude's lines here. The line "Over there in that manhole, Laertes" is original, but Laertes' response is found in this same scene.

The confrontation of Laertes and Hamlet over Ophelia's grave (V, i).

Claudius' skillful manipulation of Laertes in which he contrives to use Laertes' desire for revenge as an instrument to slay Hamlet (IV, vii).

The scene in which Osric comes to Hamlet and Horatio and conveys to them the plans for the duel (V, ii). Also the subsequent brief conversation between Hamlet and Horatio.

The actual duel (V, ii) and the subsequent carnage. The sequence and sense of the various deaths is somewhat changed.

The few references to the pistol are, of course, original, and there are one or two original lines with reference to the mechanics of the Russian roulette.

COSTUMES

HAMLET: A white linen double-breasted suit, rumpled, with a mourning band on one arm. A polo shirt and black tie, a black beret and horned-rimmed glasses. He also appears in boxer shorts that match those Claudius wears. As Ramon he wears baggy gray pants held up with loose suspenders, a leather jacket, a worker's hat, a black wig, and a false nose with glasses attached. On other occasions he adds a bowler, a straw hat, a baseball cap, and a gray hounds-tooth cape.

CLAUDIUS: Khaki military uniform with medals and a general's scrambled-egg hat. A shoulder holster with pistol, under the jacket. He also has a dress blue jacket with even more medals and a hat to match.

GERTRUDE: A filmy green negligee. A trim fuchsia cocktail dress. A long purple evening gown.

GHOST: A white union suit and sneakers; a badly burned combat helmet. Over the union suit, he will wear a military jacket and hat like that Claudius wears, a set of tails, a bowler, and a gold helmet with huge gold horns. He never wears pants, and in his first appearance wears only the union suit and the combat helmet.

HORATIO: Prisoner's stripes.

POLONIUS: Top hat and tails, black, with a scarlet diplomatic sash.

OPHELIA: A pink mini-dress and under it a green mini slip. Later a mini-cocktail dress, low cut. Later top hat and tails with black stockings.

LAERTES: A tuxedo. Later a corduroy suit with an overcoat.

ROSSENCRAFT and GILDERSTONE: Blazers and slacks in modest tones.

OSRIC: A khaki officer's uniform. Later a huge overcoat and fur hat.

GUARDS: Olive drab fatigues and combat helmets. Paratroop boots and one-way mirrored sunglasses. They are armed with .45-caliber automatics and billy-clubs. They have white dress combat helmets for the party scene and Ophelia's vaudeville number, but are generally casual and undisciplined in their dress.

NORWEGIAN CAPTAIN: A navy blue pea jacket with a fur collar, navy blue pants, and a fur hat.

PROP LIST

7 billy clubs with holsters
7 dummy .45 automatics with holsters
1 trick dueling pistol (chamber must spin to establish Russian
   roulette game and the pistol must fire or not fire on cue)
1 pistol in shoulder holster
2 starter pistols with blanks
1 cap pistol
1 coffin on wheels fitted with mattress, pillow, sheets
1 bed on wheels fitted with 2 pillows, three sheets, 1 blanket
1 telephone
1 hand mirror
   peanuts in small bag in vendor's carrying tray
   helium balloons which Hamlet sells to audience
10 flashlights
1 very large Panda bear
1 grotesque rubber hand (green or black)
1 newspaper with banner headline,
   KING STRUCK BY LIGHTNING
1 pair real handcuffs
1 pair trick handcuffs to open on cue
1 large key for trick handcuffs
   cigars
   loaded cigar

letter to Norway in heavy manila envelope
large wad of paper money
2 large photographs in frames: King Hamlet and King Claudius
each in state uniform
1 tape recorder (to look like radio) to play ghostly noises on cue
2 champagne glasses
1 packet of love letters
2 helium balloons marked KING
1 helium balloon marked QUEEN
2 straw boater hats
1 plastic garbage pail
1 push broom
1 pair trick glasses with attached false nose
1 clip-on moustache
1 rubber mouse
1 "dirty" picture
Claudius' play speech
matches
Mincing Malicho hat (a helmet with large horns, gold)
2 low sawhorses with platform (unfinished wood)
2 high sawhorses with platform (unfinished wood)
1 step-unit (unfinished wood)
3 bentwood chairs
1 whistle on chain
1 rolling "party" table or tea caddy to hold party favors and props
1 bottle of scotch with cork stopper
11 empty beer cans
streamers, horns and other party favors
1 hand buzzer
1 live beer
1 guitar
1 8mm movie camera
7 paper party hats
1 fancy goblet for the Queen
plastic recorder
1 swivel chair on castors
loose film
candle in holder, long matches

paper tablecloth

paper plates, cups, party napkins, tiny party hats, crepe paper cloth streamers

1 music box that turns on and off on cue, plays a child's tune wooden bowl with loose peanuts

paper sack with peanuts

1 electric cordless razor

1 pink parasol

2 red paper hearts on sticks

2 wire trash barrels on dollies

1 barrel lid

10 black blindfolds

bouquet of flowers

1 plastic flower

1 red wagon

1 attaché case

1 funeral wreath with **R.I.P. WILL SHAKESPEARE** on one side, a photo-portrait of Hamlet on the other